THE COUNT OF MONTE CRISTO

Alexandre Dumas

SPARK PUBLISHING

SPARKNOTES is a registered trademark of SparkNotes LLC

Spark Publishing
A Division of Barnes & Noble
120 Fifth Avenue
New York, NY 10011
www.sparknotes.com

ISBN-13: 978-1-4114-0372-7
ISBN-10: 1-4114-0372-X

Please submit changes or report errors to www.sparknotes.com/errors.

Printed in the United States.

10 9 8 7 6 5

CONTENTS

Context

ALEXANDRE DUMAS WAS BORN in 1802 in the village of Villers-Cotterêts, fifty miles northeast of Paris. His father, Thomas-Alexandre Dumas, had been a general under Napoleon, though in 1799 the two men had a falling out and never reconciled. Thomas-Alexandre never received the pay due to him as a former officer, so his family was left poor. In 1806 the elder Dumas died, and his wife and two children struggled to keep afloat. Despite the problems that Napoleon caused to the Dumas family, Alexandre remained a lifelong admirer of the former emperor. Indeed, there are strong democratic leanings evident in Dumas's literary works.

The younger Dumas was not a good student, but he had excellent handwriting. When he moved to Paris in 1823, hoping to make his fortune as an author, his lovely handwriting earned him a job as a minor clerk. Dumas spent six years as a clerk, during which time he wrote plays, conducted torrid love affairs, and lived beyond his means, until, in 1829, he had his first dramatic success, with *Henry III and His Court*. This play thrust Dumas into the limelight as one of the forerunners of the emergent French Romantic movement, which emphasized excitement, adventure, and high emotion in an attempt to rebel against the conservative climate of the Restoration period that followed the French Revolution.

Like his Romantic colleagues, Dumas believed in the principles of social equality and individual rights, and he tried to infuse his dramatic works with these principles. Dumas went further than writing about his beliefs, however. He took an active role in the Revolution of 1830, helping to capture a powder magazine at Soissons, and he was appointed organizer of the National Guard at Vendée. Encountering strong local opposition, Dumas gave up the position, refusing to act against the wishes of the majority.

Returning to the literary community of Paris, Dumas continued to write popular plays, sticking to historical works that he filled with melodrama. He also began to write travel literature, which led to a walking tour of southern France in 1834 (a tour that would later be put to use in *The Count of Monte Cristo*). In the late 1830s, Dumas began writing novels, as much for financial gain as for artistic reasons. It had become common for cheap newspapers to run novels in serial form, and if a writer was adept at writing quickly and melodramatically, as Dumas was, the financial incentives were enormous. Dumas was so good at this sort of writing that he sometimes had three or four serial novels running simultaneously. His writing soon made him the most famous Frenchman of his day, and he gained renown throughout the Western world. In 1844, the same year he published *The Three Musketeers,* Dumas began the serialization of *The Count of Monte Cristo.* He continued writing prolifically for most of his life, publishing his last novel, *The Prussian Terror,* in 1867, three years before his death.

Dumas also found the time to live like one of his dashing, dramatic, reckless heroes. He was constantly engaged in love affairs, foreign adventures, and exorbitant spending. He was also a generous man, granting money and gifts to virtually anyone who asked. Dumas's self-indulgent lifestyle and excessive generosity eventually took a toll on his finances. By the time he suffered a stroke in 1870, he was far from a rich man, despite the fact that he had earned millions of dollars in his lifetime. He died in December 1870 at the home of his son, the novelist Alexandre Dumas the younger.

Dumas's liberal borrowing from outside sources occasionally brought him accusations of plagiarism. While he lifted many of his plotlines from the works of other authors and from historical events, he molded these stories in his own characteristic way, making them his own. *The Count of Monte Cristo* is an example of the appropriation process Dumas frequently employed. His inspiration for the novel was an anecdote he read in *Mémoires historiques tirés des archives de la police de Paris,* a collection of intriguing criminal cases recorded by Jacques Peuchet, a former police archivist. The anecdote relates that in 1807, a man named François Piçaud became engaged to a pretty and wealthy girl, inspiring the envy of his friends. One of these friends, Loupian, persuaded the others to join him in denouncing Piçaud as an English spy. Though innocent of the charge, Piçaud was arrested and kept in prison for seven years. While in prison, he befriended a rich Italian cleric who left Piçaud his vast fortune when he died. Piçaud returned to Paris in 1815 as a wealthy man. Using his wealth, as well as numerous disguises, he enacted a complex plan to avenge himself on his enemies, murdering several of them. Though this real-life story has the all the essential plot elements of Dumas's novel, it lacks the fantastical, epic proportions of great melodrama. Dumas's greatest gift was his ability to grant epic proportion to existing stories.

Napoleon Bonaparte & *The Count of Monte Cristo*

The Count of Monte Cristo is a novel set firmly in history, with many key plot points based on external political events. The key figure in French politics during the first quarter of the nineteenth century was Napoleon Bonaparte, who, though he does not appear in the novel, plays such a significant role that he can almost be counted as one of the major characters. Napoleon was a general who rose to prominence during the French Revolution, which occurred in 1789. He saved the revolutionary government from an angry mob and led the French army to victories over Austria, Italy, and Egypt, claiming all of these lands for France. In 1799, Napoleon led a coup against the existing government of France and formed a consulate, installing himself as its dictatorial leader.

In 1804, Napoleon revised the constitution he had written several years earlier, and the French senate voted him emperor of all of the vast lands he had conquered. Napoleon remained widely beloved by the people, largely because in all the lands he conquered, he abolished serfdom and feudalism and guaranteed basic human rights. He simplified the court system, took steps to make education universally available, and standardized national codes of law to ensure that the rights and liberties won during the French Revolution—equality before the law and freedom of religion—could not be taken away.

In 1814, dogged by an increasing number of enemies and looming military defeat, Napoleon was forced to abdicate his throne. He was exiled to the Mediterranean island of Elba, where Edmond Dantès finds him at the beginning of *The Count of Monte Cristo*. In March 1815, Napoleon escaped from Elba, secretly sailed to France, and marched on Paris, defeating the royal troops. It is information about this return to power that is contained in the letter Dantès is caught conveying to Paris.

After his return to power, Napoleon advocated an even more liberal constitution than the one he had first instituted. After a brief period, however, Napoleon was forced to make a preemptive strike against encroaching enemies, and he met defeat at the Battle of Waterloo. Parisian crowds, supporting Napoleon as fervently as ever, begged him to keep fighting. Several key politicians withdrew their support, however, and Napoleon surrendered. His short second reign is known as the Hundred Days. With Napoleon defeated, France fell back into the hands of the ultraconservative Louis XVIII. Napoleon was exiled to the South Atlantic island of Saint Helena, where he lived until his death in 1821. However, Napoleon's absence from France only intensified his mythic status, and he became an even greater hero than at any time he was actually present in France. Dumas's idealization of Napoleon is not at all rare, as Napoleon, in his time, was hailed as though he were a patron saint of France.

Plot Overview

AT THE AGE OF NINETEEN, Edmond Dantès seems to have the perfect life. He is about to become the captain of a ship, he is engaged to a beautiful and kind young woman, Mercédès, and he is well liked by almost everyone who knows him. This perfect life, however, stirs up dangerous jealousy among some of Dantès's so-called friends. Danglars, the treasurer of Dantès's ship, envies Dantès's early career success; Fernand Mondego is in love with Dantès's fiancée and so covets his amorous success; his neighbor Caderousse is simply envious that Dantès is so much luckier in life than he is.

Together, these three men draft a letter accusing Dantès of treason. There is some truth to their accusations: as a favor to his recently deceased captain, Dantès is carrying a letter from Napoleon to a group of Bonapartist sympathizers in Paris. Though Dantès himself has no political leanings, the undertaking is enough to implicate him for treason. On the day of his wedding, Dantès is arrested for his alleged crimes.

The deputy public prosecutor, Villefort, sees through the plot to frame Dantès and is prepared to set him free. At the last moment, though, Dantès jeopardizes his freedom by revealing the name of the man to whom he is supposed to deliver Napoleon's letter. The man, Noirtier, is Villefort's father. Terrified that any public knowledge of his father's treasonous activities will thwart his own ambitions, Villefort decides to send Dantès to prison for life. Despite the entreaties of Monsieur Morrel, Dantès's kind and honest boss, Dantès is sent to the infamous Château d'If, where the most dangerous political prisoners are kept.

While in prison, Dantès meets Abbé Faria, an Italian priest and intellectual, who has been jailed for his political views. Faria teaches Dantès history, science, philosophy, and languages, turning him into a well-educated man. Faria also bequeaths to Dantès a large treasure hidden on the island of Monte Cristo, and he tells him how to find it should he ever escape. When Faria dies, Dantès hides himself in the abbé's shroud, thinking that he will be buried and then dig his way out. Instead, Dantès is thrown into the sea, and is able to cut himself loose and swim to freedom.

Dantès travels to Monte Cristo and finds Faria's enormous treasure. He considers his fortune a gift from God, given to him for the sole purpose of rewarding those who have tried to help him and, more important, punishing those who have hurt him. Disguising himself as an Italian priest who answers to the name of Abbé Busoni, he travels back to Marseilles and visits Caderousse, who is now struggling to make a living as an innkeeper. From Caderousse he learns the details of the plot to frame him. In addition, Dantès learns that his father has died of grief in his absence and that Mercédès has married Fernand Mondego. Most frustrating, he learns that both Danglars and Mondego have become rich and powerful and are living happily in Paris. As a reward for this information, and for Caderousse's apparent regret over the part he played in Dantès's downfall, Dantès gives Caderousse a valuable diamond. Before leaving Marseilles, Dantès anonymously saves Morrel from financial ruin.

Ten years later, Dantès emerges in Rome, calling himself the Count of Monte Cristo. He seems to be all knowing and unstoppable. In Rome Dantès ingratiates himself to Albert de Morcerf, son of Fernand Mondego and Mercédès, by saving him from bandits. In return for the favor, Albert introduces Dantès to Parisian society. None of his old cohorts recognize the mysterious count as Edmond Dantès, though Mercédès does. Dantès is thus able to insinuate himself effortlessly into the lives of Danglars, Mondego, and Villefort. Armed with damning knowledge about each of them that he has gathered over the past decade, Dantès sets an elaborate scheme of revenge into motion.

Mondego, now known as the Count de Morcerf, is the first to be punished. Dantès exposes Morcerf's darkest secret: Morcerf made his fortune by betraying his former patron, the Greek vizier Ali Pacha, and he then sold Ali Pacha's wife and daughter into slavery. Ali Pacha's daughter, Haydée, who has lived with Dantès ever since he bought her freedom seven years earlier, testifies against Morcerf in front of the senate, irreversibly ruining his good name. Ashamed by Morcerf's treachery, Albert and Mercédès flee, leaving their tainted fortune behind. Morcerf commits suicide.

Villefort's punishment comes slowly and in several stages. Dantès first takes advantage of Madame de Villefort's murderous intent, subtly tutoring her in the uses of poison. As Madame de Villefort wreaks her havoc, killing off each member of the household in turn, Dantès plants the seeds for yet another public exposé. In court, it is revealed that Villefort is guilty of attempted infanticide, as he tried to bury his illegitimate baby while it was still alive. Believing that everyone he loves is dead and knowing that he will soon have to answer severe criminal charges, Villefort goes insane.

For his revenge on Danglars, Dantès simply plays upon his enemy's greed. He opens various false credit accounts with Danglars that cost him vast amounts of money. He also manipulates Danglars's unfaithful and dishonest wife, costing Danglars more money, and helps Danglars's daughter, Eugénie, run away with her female companion. Finally, when Danglars is nearly broke and about to flee without paying any of his creditors, Dantès has the Italian bandit Luigi Vampa kidnap him and relieve him of his remaining money. Dantès spares Danglars's life, but leaves him penniless.

Meanwhile, as these acts of vengeance play out, Dantès also tries to complete one more act of goodness. Dantès wishes to help the brave and honorable Maximilian Morrel, the son of the kind shipowner, so he hatches an elaborate plot to save Maximilian's fiancée, Valentine Villefort, from her murderous stepmother, to ensure that the couple will be truly happy forever. Dantès gives Valentine a pill that makes her appear dead and then carries her off to the island of Monte Cristo. For a month Dantès allows Maximilian to believe that Valentine is dead, which causes Maximilian to long for death himself. Dantès then reveals that Valentine is alive. Having known the depths of despair, Maximilian is now able to experience the heights of ecstasy. Dantès too ultimately finds happiness, when he allows himself to fall in love with the adoring and beautiful Haydée.

CHARACTER LIST

EDMOND DANTÈS AND ALIASES

> NOTE: *This SparkNote refers to Dantès by his given name through Chapter 30, after which it generally refers to him as Monte Cristo.*

Edmond Dantès The protagonist of the novel. Dantès is an intelligent, honest, and loving man who turns bitter and vengeful after he is framed for a crime he does not commit. When Dantès finds himself free and enormously wealthy, he takes it upon himself to act as the agent of Providence, rewarding those who have helped him in his plight and punishing those responsible for his years of agony.

The Count of Monte Cristo The identity Dantès assumes when he emerges from prison and inherits his vast fortune. As a result, the Count of Monte Cristo is usually associated with a coldness and bitterness that comes from an existence based solely on vengeance.

Lord Wilmore The identity of an eccentric English nobleman that Dantès assumes when committing acts of random generosity. Lord Wilmore contrasts sharply with Monte Cristo, who is associated with Dantès's acts of bitterness and cruelty. Appropriately, Monte Cristo cites Lord Wilmore as one of his enemies.

Abbé Busoni Another of Dantès's false personas. The disguise of Abbé Busoni, an Italian priest, helps Dantès gain the trust of the people whom the count wants to manipulate because the name connotes religious authority.

Sinbad the Sailor The name Dantès uses as the signature for his anonymous gift to Morrel. Sinbad the Sailor is also the persona Dantès adopts during his time in Italy.

OTHER CHARACTERS

Mercédès Dantès's beautiful and good fiancée. Though Mercédès marries another man, Fernand Mondego, while Dantès is in prison, she never stops loving Dantès. Mercédès is one of the few whom Dantès both punishes (for her disloyalty) and rewards (for her enduring love and underlying goodness).

Abbé Faria A priest and brilliant thinker whom Dantès meets in prison. Abbé Faria becomes Dantès's intellectual father: during their many years as prisoners, he teaches Dantès history, science, art, and many languages. He then bequeaths to Dantès his vast hidden fortune. Abbé Faria is the most important catalyst in Dantès's transformation into the vengeful Count of Monte Cristo.

Fernand Mondego Dantès's rival for Mercédès's affections. Mondego helps in framing Dantès for treason and then marries Mercédès himself when Dantès is imprisoned. Through acts of treachery Mondego becomes a wealthy and powerful man and takes on the name of the Count de Morcerf. He is the first victim of Dantès's vengeance.

Baron Danglars A greedy, envious cohort of Mondego. Danglars hatches the plot to frame Dantès for treason. Like Mondego, he becomes wealthy and powerful, but loses everything when Monte Cristo takes his revenge. Danglars's obsession with the accumulation of wealth makes him an easy target for Monte Cristo, who has seemingly limitless wealth on hand to exact his revenge.

Caderousse A lazy, drunk, and greedy man. Caderousse is present when the plot to frame Dantès is hatched, but he does not take an active part in the crime. Unlike Danglars and Mondego, Caderousse never finds his fortune, instead making his living through petty crime and the occasional murder.

Gérard de Villefort The blindly ambitious public prosecutor responsible for sentencing Dantès to life in prison. Like the others, Villefort eventually receives punishment from Dantès. Villefort stands out as Monte Cristo's biggest opposition, as he employs his own power to judge people and mete out punishments.

Monsieur Morrel The kind, honest shipowner who was once Dantès's boss. Morrel does everything in his power to free Dantès from prison and tries to save Dantès's father from death. When Dantès emerges from prison, he discovers that Morrel is about to descend into financial ruin, so he carries out an elaborate plot to save his one true friend.

Louis Dantès Dantès's father. Grief-stricken, Louis Dantès starves himself to death when Dantès is imprisoned. It is primarily for his father's death that Dantès seeks vengeance.

Maximilian Morrel The son of Monsieur Morrel. Brave and honorable like his father, Maximilian becomes Dantès's primary beneficiary. Maximilian and his love, Valentine, survive to the end of the story as two good and happy people, personally unaffected by the vices of power, wealth, and position.

Albert de Morcerf The son of Fernand Mondego and Mercédès. Unlike his father, Albert is brave, honest, and kind. Mercédès's devotion to both Albert and Dantès allows Monte Cristo to realize her unchanging love for him and causes him to think more deeply about his sole desire for revenge.

Valentine Villefort Villefort's saintly and beautiful daughter. Like Maximilian Morrel, her true love, she falls under Dantès's protection.

Noirtier Villefort's father. Once a powerful French revolutionary, Noirtier is brilliant and willful, even when paralyzed by a stroke. He proves a worthy opponent to his son's selfish ambitions.

Haydée The daughter of Ali Pacha, the vizier of the Greek state of Yanina. Haydée is sold into slavery after her father is betrayed by Mondego and murdered. Dantès purchases Haydée's freedom and watches her grow into adulthood, eventually falling in love with her.

Signor Bertuccio Dantès's steward. Though Bertuccio is loyal and adept, Dantès chooses him as his steward not for his personal qualities but because of his vendetta against Villefort.

Benedetto The illegitimate son of Villefort and Madame Danglars. Though raised lovingly by Bertuccio and Bertuccio's widowed sister-in-law, Benedetto nonetheless turns to a life of brutality and crime. Handsome, charming, and a wonderful liar, Benedetto plays the part of Andrea Cavalcanti in one of Dantès's elaborate revenge schemes.

Madame d'Villefort Villefort's murderous wife. Devoted wholly to her son Edward, Madame d'Villefort turns to crime in order to ensure his fortune.

Julie Herbaut The daughter of Monsieur Morrel and sister of Maximilian. Angelically good and blissfully in love, Julie and her husband, Emmanuel, prove to Monte Cristo that it is possible to be truly satisfied with one's life.

Emmanuel Herbaut Julie's husband. Emmanuel is just as noble and perpetually happy as his wife, Julie.

Madame Danglars Danglars's wife. Greedy, conniving, and disloyal, Madame Danglars engages in a never-ending string of love affairs that help bring her husband to the brink of financial ruin.

Eugénie Danglars The Danglars' daughter. A brilliant musician, Eugénie longs for her independence and despises men. On the eve of her wedding, she flees for Italy with her true love, Louise d'Armilly.

Louise d'Armilly Eugénie Danglars's music teacher and constant companion.

Lucien Debray The secretary to the French minister of the interior. Debray illegally leaks government secrets to his lover, Madame Danglars, so that she can invest wisely with her husband's money.

Ali Dantès's mute Nubian slave. Ali is amazingly adept with all sorts of weapons.

Luigi Vampa A famous Roman bandit. Vampa is indebted to Dantès for once setting him free, and he puts himself at the service of Dantès's vengeful ends.

Major Cavalcanti A poor and crooked man whom Dantès resurrects as a phony Italian nobleman.

Edward d'Villefort The Villeforts' spoiled son. Edward is an innocent victim of Dantès's elaborate revenge scheme.

Beauchamp A well-known journalist and good friend to Albert de Morcerf.

Franz d'Epinay Another good friend to Albert de Morcerf. D'Epinay is the unwanted fiancé of Valentine Villefort.

Marquis of Saint-Méran The father of Villefort's first wife, who dies shortly after her wedding day.

Marquise of Saint-Méran The wife of the Marquis of Saint-Méran.

Jacopo A smuggler who helps Dantès win his freedom. When Jacopo proves his selfless loyalty, Dantès rewards him by buying the poor man his own ship and crew.

Ali Pacha   A Greek nationalist leader whom Mondego betrays. This betrayal leads to Ali Pacha's murder at the hands of the Turks and the seizure of his kingdom. Ali Pacha's wife and his daughter, Haydée, are sold into slavery.

Baron of Château-Renaud   An aristocrat and diplomat. Château-Renaud is nearly killed in battle in Constantinople, but Maximilian Morrel saves him at the last second. Château-Renaud introduces Maximilian into Parisian society, which leads to Maximilian and Dantès crossing paths.

Peppino   An Italian shepherd who has been arrested and sentenced to death for the crime of being an accomplice to bandits, when he merely provided them with food. Monte Cristo buys Peppino his freedom.

Countess G—   A beautiful Italian aristocrat who suspects that Monte Cristo is a vampire.

ANALYSIS OF MAJOR CHARACTERS

EDMOND DANTÈS

Before his imprisonment, Edmond Dantès is a kind, innocent, honest, and loving man. Though naturally intelligent, he is a man of few opinions, living his life instinctively by a traditional code of ethics that impels him to honor his superiors, care dutifully for his aging father, and treat his fellow man generously. Dantès is filled with positive feeling, admiring his boss, Monsieur Morrel; loving his father; adoring his fiancée, Mercédès; and even attempting to think kindly of men who clearly dislike him.

While in prison, however, Dantès undergoes a great change. He becomes bitter and vengeful as he obsesses over the wrongs committed against him. When his companion, Abbé Faria, dies, so too does Dantès's only remaining deep connection to another human being. Dantès loses the capacity to feel any emotion other than hatred for those who have harmed him and gratitude toward those who have tried to help him. He moves through the world like an outsider, disconnected from any human community and interested only in carrying out his mission as the agent of Providence. It is not until Dantès finds love again, in a relationship with Haydée, that he is able to reconnect to his own humanity and begin to live humanly again.

DANGLARS

A greedy and ruthless man, Danglars cares only for his personal fortune. He has no qualms about sacrificing others for the sake of his own welfare, and he goes through life shrewdly calculating ways to turn other people's misfortunes to his own advantage. Danglars's betrayal of Dantès starts him on the path to utter disregard for other people's lives, but this betrayal is not the cruelest of his acts. Danglars abandons his wife and attempts to sell his own daughter, Eugénie, into a loveless and miserable marriage for three million francs.

Though he manages to claw his way into a position of great wealth and power, Danglars's greed grows as he grows richer, and his lust for money continues to drive all his actions in the two decades that the novel spans. Even when faced with the prospect of starvation, Danglars prefers to keep his fortune rather than pay an exorbitant price for food. Finally, Danglars relents in his pathological avarice, allowing that he would give all his remaining money just to remain alive. Only after Danglars repents for the evil he has done does Dantès consider Danglars redeemed and pardon him.

MERCÉDÈS

Resigned to the blows that fate deals her, Mercédès acts as a foil to her onetime fiancé, Dantès. Though she is a good and kind woman, her timidness and passivity lead her to betray her beloved and marry another man, Mondego. Mercédès remains miserable for the rest of her life, despising herself for her weakness and longing for Dantès, whom she has never stopped loving. Yet, for all her avowed weakness and fear, Mercédès proves herself capable of great courage on three occasions: first, when she approaches Dantès to beg for her the life of her son, Albert; second, when she reveals her husband's wickedness in order to save Dantès's life; and third, when she abandons her wealth, unwilling to live off a fortune that has been tainted by misdeeds. At the end of the novel, Mercédès is left with nothing to live for, aside from the hope that Albert might somehow improve his own life. She is the character whose suffering is the most complete, despite the fact that there are others who bear far more guilt.

CADEROUSSE

Caderousse exemplifies human dissatisfaction, helping to illustrate that happiness depends more on attitude than on external circumstances. Though fate—or, more precisely, Dantès—treats Caderousse fairly well, he is never truly satisfied with his life. No matter how much he has, Caderousse always feels that he deserves more. With each improvement in his position, Caderousse's desires only increase. He is pained by the good fortune of his friends, and his envy festers into hatred and ultimately into crime. Not only covetous but also lazy and dishonest, Caderousse consistently resorts to dishonorable means in order to acquire what he wants, thieving and even murdering in order to better his own position. Ultimately, Caderousse's unending greed catches up with him, and he dies while trying to rob Monte Cristo.

THEMES, MOTIFS & SYMBOLS

THEMES

Themes are the fundamental and often universal ideas explored in a literary work.

THE LIMITS OF HUMAN JUSTICE

Edmond Dantès takes justice into his own hands because he is dismayed by the limitations of society's criminal justice system. Societal justice has allowed his enemies to slip through the cracks, going unpunished for the heinous crimes they have committed against him. Moreover, even if his enemies' crimes were uncovered, Dantès does not believe that their punishment would be true justice. Though his enemies have caused him years of emotional anguish, the most that they themselves would be forced to suffer would be a few seconds of pain, followed by death.

Considering himself an agent of Providence, Dantès aims to carry out divine justice where he feels human justice has failed. He sets out to punish his enemies as he believes they should be punished: by destroying all that is dear to them, just as they have done to him. Yet what Dantès ultimately learns, as he sometimes wreaks havoc in the lives of the innocent as well as the guilty, is that justice carried out by human beings is inherently limited. The limits of such justice lie in the limits of human beings themselves. Lacking God's omniscience and omnipotence, human beings are simply not capable of—or justified in—carrying out the work of Providence. Dumas's final message in this epic work of crime and punishment is that human beings must simply resign themselves to allowing God to reward and punish—when and how God sees fit.

RELATIVE VERSUS ABSOLUTE HAPPINESS

A great deal separates the sympathetic from the unsympathetic characters in *The Count of Monte Cristo*. The trait that is most consistently found among the sympathetic characters and lacking among the unsympathetic is the ability to assess one's circumstances in such a way as to feel satisfaction and happiness with one's life. In his parting message to Maximilian, Dantès claims that "[t]here is neither happiness nor misery in the world; there is only the comparison of one state with another, nothing more." In simpler terms, what separates the good from the bad in *The Count of Monte Cristo* is that the good appreciate the good things they have, however small, while the bad focus on what they lack.

Dantès's enemies betray him out of an envy that arises from just this problem: despite the blessings these men have in their own lives, Dantès's relatively superior position sends them into a rage of dissatisfaction. Caderousse exemplifies this psychological deficiency, finding fault in virtually every positive circumstance that life throws his way. Caderousse could easily be a happy man, as he is healthy, clever, and reasonably well off, yet he is unable to view his circumstances in such a way as to feel happy. At the other end of the spectrum are Julie and Emmanuel Herbaut—they are fully capable of feeling happiness, even in the face of pressing poverty and other hardships. The Dantès of the early chapters, perfectly thrilled with the small happiness that God has granted him, provides another example of the good and easily satisfied man, while the Dantès of later chapters, who has emerged from prison unable to find happiness unless he exacts his complicated revenge, provides an example of the bad and unsatisfiable man.

LOVE VERSUS ALIENATION

Dantès declares himself an exile from humanity during the years in which he carries out his elaborate scheme of revenge. He feels cut off not only from all countries, societies, and individuals but also from normal human emotions. Dantès is unable to experience joy, sorrow, or excitement; in fact, the only emotions he is capable of feeling are vengeful hatred and occasional gratitude. It is plausible that Dantès's extreme social isolation and narrow range of feeling are simply the result of his obsession with his role as the agent of Providence. It is not difficult to imagine that a decade-long devotion to a project like Dantès's might take a dramatic toll on one's psychology.

Yet Dantès's alienation from humanity is not solely due to his obsessive lust for revenge but also to his lack of love for any living person. Though he learns of his enemies' treachery years before he escapes from prison, his alienation from humanity begins to take hold only when Abbé Faria dies. Until Faria's death, Dantès's love for Faria keeps him connected to his own humanity, by keeping the humanizing emotion of love alive within him. When Dantès learns that his father is dead and that Mercédès has married another man, his alienation is complete. There are no longer any living people whom he loves, and he loses hold of any humanizing force.

This humanizing force eventually returns when Dantès falls in love with Haydée. This relationship reconciles Dantès to his humanity and enables him to feel real emotion once again. In a triumphant declaration of emotion, he says to Haydée, "through you I again connect myself with life, through you I shall suffer, through you rejoice." Dantès's overcomes his alienation, both from society and from his own humanity, through his love of another human being.

MOTIFS

Motifs are recurring structures, contrasts, and literary devices that can help to develop and inform the text's major themes.

NAMES

The constant changing of characters' names in *The Count of Monte Cristo* signifies deeper changes within the characters themselves. Like the God of the Old Testament, Dantès assumes a host of different names, each associated with a different role in his schemes as the agent of Providence. He calls himself Abbé Busoni when standing in judgment, Lord Wilmore when engaging in acts of excessive generosity, and Monte Cristo when assuming the role of avenging angel. That Dantès possesses so many identities suggests that he lacks a true center.

Villefort also changes his name, though for different reasons: he refuses to adopt his father's title of Noirtier, a name closely associated with the despised Bonapartist party. Villefort's choice of names signifies both his political opportunism and his willingness to sacrifice ruthlessly those close to him for his own personal gain. Fernand Mondego's change of name to Count de Morcerf is, on one level, merely a sign of his ascent into the realm of power and prestige. Yet, since Mondego pretends that Morcerf is an old family name rather than merely a title he has purchased, the name-change is also a symbol of his fundamental dishonesty. Mercédès also undergoes a change of name, becoming Countess de Morcerf. This change in name, however, as we learn when Mercédès proves her enduring goodness, does not accompany a fundamental change in character. Instead, her name-change merely emphasizes her connection to her husband, Dantès's rival, and, by association, her disloyalty to

Dantès. Only Benedetto's change of name, to Andrea Cavalcanti, seems to signify nothing deeper than the fact that he is assuming a false identity. All of the other name changes in the novel are external signals of internal changes of character or role.

SUICIDE

Many characters in *The Count of Monte Cristo*—Dantès, Monsieur Morrel, Maximilian Morrel, Haydée, Fernand Mondego, Madame d'Villefort, and Albert de Morcerf—contemplate or even carry out suicide during the course of the novel. Dumas presents the act of suicide as an honorable and reasonable response to any devastating situation. As in much Romantic literature, suicide in *The Count of Monte Cristo* is most closely linked with failed romantic relationships.

In fact, eagerness to take one's own life for the sake of a beloved is held up as one of the only sure signs of absolute devotion. Monte Cristo is convinced that Maximilian loves Valentine, for instance, only when he sees that Maximilian sincerely wants to die when confronted with her loss. Likewise, Monte Cristo believes that Haydée loves him only when she swears that she would take her life if he abandoned her. The frequency with which suicide is mentioned or contemplated by characters might seem to reflect a cavalier attitude toward this most serious of acts. However, suicide is clearly regarded as a serious action: Dantès gravely warns Maximilian not to take his life if there is anything in the world that he regrets leaving. The characters in the novel are not arrogant about life—they simply live it melodramatically, finding the world devoid of hope and meaning on a fairly regular basis.

POLITICS

The Count of Monte Cristo is a historical novel, with key plot elements drawn from real historic events. Politics, therefore, play a significant role in the novel, particularly in branding certain characters good or bad. All of the major sympathetic characters are somehow connected to the democratic ideals of the Bonapartist party, from Morrel and Noirtier, who were once ardent fighters in the Bonapartist cause, to Dantès, who emerges as a champion for individual rights. Likewise, in his wooing of Valentine, Maximilian fights for social equality, another Bonapartist ideal. Many of the major unsympathetic characters, by contrast, are overwhelmingly associated with the oppressive, aristocratic royalists, such as Morcerf and Villefort. Others are simply self-serving capitalist opportunists, such as Danglars, responsible for ushering in the soul-deadening age of the Industrial Revolution. In this sense, Dumas does not assign political allegiances arbitrarily, but uses them as windows into the souls of his characters.

SYMBOLS

Symbols are objects, characters, figures, and colors used to represent abstract ideas or concepts.

THE SEA

When Dantès escapes from prison, he plunges into the ocean, experiencing a second baptism and a renewed dedication of his soul to God. He has suffered a metaphorical death while in prison: the death of his innocent, loving self. Dantès emerges as a bitter and hateful man, bent on carrying out revenge on his enemies. He is washed in the waters that lead him to freedom, and his rebirth as a man transformed is complete. The sea continues to figure prominently in the novel even after this symbolic baptism. Considering himself a citizen of no land, Dantès spends much of his time on the ocean, traveling the world in his yacht. The sea seems to beckon constantly to Dantès, a skilled sailor, offering him perpetual escape and solitude.

THE RED SILK PURSE

First used by Monsieur Morrel in his attempt to save the life of Dantès's father, Dantès later uses the red silk purse when he is saving Morrel's life. The red purse becomes the physical symbol of the connection between good deed and reward. Morrel recognizes the purse and deduces the connection between the good deed performed on his behalf and the good deed he once performed himself. Morrel concludes that Dantès must be his savior, surmising that he is working from beyond the grave. Morrel's daughter, Julie, then emphasizes the symbolic power of the purse by keeping it constantly on display as a relic of her father's miraculous salvation.

THE ELIXIR

Dantès's potent potion seems to have the power both to kill and to bring to life, a power that Dantès comes to believe in too strongly. His overestimation of the elixir's power reflects his overestimation of his own power, his delusion that he is almost godlike, and his assertion that he has the right and capacity to act as the agent of Providence. It is significant that, when faced with Edward's corpse,

Dantès thinks first to use his elixir to bring the boy to life. Of course, the elixir is not powerful enough to bring the dead to life, just as Dantès himself is not capable of accomplishing divine feats. The power to grant life—like the power to carry out ultimate retribution and justice—lies solely in God's province. It is when Dantès acknowledges the limits of his elixir that he realizes his own limitations as a human being.

SUMMARY & ANALYSIS

CHAPTERS 1–5

CHAPTER 1: THE ARRIVAL AT MARSEILLES

In the port of Marseilles, France, an eager crowd watches as a ship called the *Pharaon* pulls into dock. The ship's owner, Monsieur Morrel, is greeted with sad news: the ship's captain has died at sea. The nineteen-year-old first mate, Edmond Dantès, reassures Morrel that despite the loss of the captain, the trip went smoothly and all the cargo arrived safely. Morrel is impressed with the young man's performance as temporary captain.

Danglars, the ship's supercargo, who is responsible for all financial matters, attempts to undermine Morrel's good opinion of Dantès. Morrel boards the ship and Danglars tells him that Dantès forced the ship to stop at the Isle of Elba, which cost them precious time. When Morrel confronts Dantès with this accusation, Dantès explains that he stopped the ship at Elba in order to carry out his captain's dying request: to deliver a package to an exiled grand-marshal, Maréchal Bertrand. He says that while he was on the island he spoke with Napoleon, the deposed emperor of France.

With this matter cleared up, Morrel asks Dantès for his opinion of Danglars. Dantès answers honestly, explaining that he has a personal dislike for Danglars but that Danglars does his work very well. Morrel approves of Dantès's behavior at Elba, of his honest assessment of an enemy, and of his character in general. Morrel declares that after he consults with his partner, Dantès will be named the new captain of the *Pharaon*, despite his young age. Dantès is ecstatic, while Danglars is beside himself with envy.

CHAPTER 2: FATHER AND SON

Leaving the docks, Dantès goes straight to see his father. He is shocked by the old man's physical deterioration and soon discovers its cause: his father has been starving for the past few months. Though Dantès left his father with 200 francs, the tailor Caderousse demanded that the elder Dantès pay him a debt that his son owed, which left the old man with only sixty francs on which to live. Dantès tells his father the good news of his promotion and hands him a modest pile of gold, telling him to buy himself all the provisions he needs.

Caderousse then enters the small room to welcome Dantès home. Dantès receives Caderousse politely, telling himself "he is a neighbour who has done us a service . . . so he's welcome." Caderousse has already heard the news of Dantès's promotion and congratulates him. Caderousse then leaves the father and son and goes downstairs, where Danglars is waiting for him. The two men discuss their dislike for Dantès and accuse him of being arrogant. Caderousse reveals that Dantès's good luck might be about to change: the woman he loves, Mercédès, has been seen in the company of another man. Danglars and Caderousse, hoping for the worst, decide to wait by the road near Mercédès's house, in order to determine whether Dantès has really been jilted.

Chapter 3: The Catalans

As expected, Dantès next goes to visit Mercédès, a beautiful girl who belongs to the Spanish community of Catalans. He finds Mercédès in the company of Fernand Mondego, her lovestruck cousin, who has been trying for years to make her his wife. Mercédès welcomes Dantès with a passionate embrace, and Fernand stalks off, enraged. Fernand passes Danglars and Caderousse drinking wine by the side of the road, and they call him over. As the three men drink together, Danglars and Caderousse try to whip Fernand up into a frenzy of envy and anger much like their own. Dantès and Mercédès appear, blissfully oblivious to the malice directed toward them. The couple tells Fernand, Caderousse, and Danglars that they plan to be married the next day because Dantès must travel to Paris to fulfill the last commission of his dead captain. Though Dantès does not state explicitly why he is going to Paris, Danglars suspects Dantès is delivering a letter that has been entrusted to him by Napoleon to Bonapartist plotters—supporters of Napoleon who are helping him plan to overthrow the French government. The allusion to the letter sparks an evil idea in Danglars's mind.

Chapter 4: The Plotters

Danglars and Fernand plot Dantès's downfall as Caderousse descends deep into intoxication. Fernand is unwilling to kill Dantès, since Mercédès has promised to commit suicide should Dantès die. Danglars suggests that they should have him imprisoned instead. Danglars drafts a letter informing the public prosecutor that Dantès is bearing a letter from Napoleon to the Bonapartist Committee in Paris. Caderousse protests against this defamation of Dantès's character, so Danglars makes a show of tossing the letter into a corner, telling Caderousse that he is merely jesting. Danglars then leads Caderousse away, and Fernand, as expected, retrieves the letter and plans to mail it.

CHAPTER 5: THE BETROTHAL FEAST

In the middle of Dantès and Mercédès's betrothal feast, royal guards burst in and arrest Dantès. Everyone is confused, especially Dantès, who has done nothing wrong, as far as he knows. Danglars offers to take over duties as captain of the *Pharaon* until Dantès is released, and Morrel gratefully accepts this offer.

ANALYSIS: CHAPTERS 1–5

From the opening of *The Count of Monte Cristo*, the hero, Edmond Dantès, comes across as a model of honesty, competence, and innocence. Despite his youth, he is an effective leader to his sailors. He is devoted to his aging father and to his young fiancée. Perhaps most admirable, Dantès is capable of overlooking his personal dislike for Danglars, Caderousse, and Fernand, and he treats all of them fairly and civilly. When Morrel asks Dantès to evaluate Danglars's work on the ship, Dantès could easily ruin his enemy's career with a mean word. Yet he chooses to put aside his personal feelings and honestly evaluates Danglars on a professional level, noting his competence as the ship's financier. Similarly, rather than rebuke Caderousse for mistreating his father, Dantès politely welcomes him into his home and offers to lend him money. Dantès even manages to curb his ill will toward Fernand, his rival for Mercédès affections. Dantès is loyal to those he loves and sees the best in those who are flawed. These traits elevate him above any of the other characters introduced so far.

While Dantès sits atop the pedestal of honesty and generosity, his three enemies could not be further from it. Unaware of Dantès's kindness and tolerance, they have convinced themselves that he is unbearably arrogant. When Dantès exults in his good luck, the other men feel injury to their own egos. Viewing Dantès's joy through the prism of their envy, they consider it to be a sign of arrogance. Dumas is careful to mention several times that Dantès is beloved by all the sailors who work under him. This fondness suggests that Dantès is extremely likable and that those who perceive arrogance on his part must have other reasons—such as their own insecurities—for this perception. Actually, only two of the enemies, Caderousse and Danglars, actually dislike Dantès at this point; Fernand's hatred of Dantès, by contrast, does not stem from any willful misreading of

Dantès's character. Fernand simply dislikes Dantès because he is the main obstacle to his own happiness with Mercédès. Dumas sets these three grudging men up as foils—characters whose attitudes or emotions contrast with and thereby accentuate those of another character—to the noble-hearted Dantès.

Though the three men all participate in Dantès's downfall, they are each guilty of a different crime that corresponds to their different attributes and relationships to Dantès. Dumas clearly portrays Danglars as the most villainous of Dantès's three enemies, the only one who acts on a premeditated plan and the only one who acts rationally and coolly toward his designs. Perhaps most important, since Danglars is the only one who suspects the contents of the letter Dantès is carrying, he is the only one who understands the ramifications of the accusations planned against Dantès. Fernand's crime, on the other hand, is an impetuous crime of passion. Gripped with the overwhelming desire to have Mercédès for himself, Fernand takes Danglars's bait and mails the letter. Different still, Caderousse is merely guilty of cowardice and weakness. He is not an active participant in drafting or mailing the letter. Yet, though Caderousse knows Dantès's motives regarding the letter are innocent, he says nothing in Dantès's defense when he is arrested. Though Caderousse feels pity for Dantès as well as guilt over his part in the crime, he is too fearful of implicating himself and chooses to remain quiet and let an innocent man go to prison. Danglars's clear, calculating ambition, Fernand's impetuous criminality, and Caderousse's cowardice and spinelessness remain the characteristics that define these three men throughout the novel.

CHAPTERS 6–14

CHAPTER 6: THE DEPUTY PROCUREUR

In another part of town, a very different betrothal feast is taking place. This feast is in honor of an aristocratic couple: the young daughter of the Marquis of Saint-Méran and her fiancé, Gérard de Villefort, the deputy public prosecutor of Marseilles. Villefort, we learn during the course of the lunch conversation, is the son of a prominent Bonapartist. In the wake of Napoleon's defeat and the subsequent reinstatement of King Louis XVIII, Villefort, an ambitious young man, has decided to ally himself with the royalists. He renounces his father and his father's politics, and swears to the assembled guests that he will brutally punish any Bonapartist sympathizer who falls into his hands. The betrothal feast is interrupted when Villefort is called away to deal with a Bonapartist plot that has just been uncovered.

Chapter 7: The Examination

After dismissing Morrel's efforts to intercede on his employee's behalf, Villefort enters his office and finds the accused plotter, Edmond Dantès. He confronts Dantès with the allegations against him. Dantès admits that he is carrying a letter to Paris and that the letter was entrusted to him by Napoleon. He pleads innocent, however, to any political involvement, explaining that he is merely carrying out the dying wish of his ship's captain. Dantès announces that he has no opinions other than his love for his father, his love for Mercédès, and his admiration for Monsieur Morrel.

Villefort takes a liking to Dantès's open, sincere character and is planning to let him go free until Dantès unwittingly lets slip the name of the man to whom the Bonapartist letter is addressed. The intended recipient is a man named Noirtier—Villefort's father. Terrified that word of his father's treasonous activities could leak out and damage his family name, Villefort decides that he must send Dantès away forever.

Chapter 8: The Château d'If

Villefort has Dantès locked away in the Château d'If, a notorious prison reserved for the most dangerous political prisoners. There, Dantès demands to see the governor and violently threatens the guard when he is refused this privilege. As punishment, Dantès is sent down into the dungeon, where the insane prisoners are kept. The guard tells Dantès about one particular prisoner in the dungeon, a man who constantly promises the guards millions of francs in exchange for his liberation.

Chapter 9: The Evening of the Betrothal

Villefort returns to his fiancée's home and announces that he must leave for Paris. He confides to his father-in-law that if he can only reach the king in time, his fortune will be made. On his way out, Villefort encounters Mercédès, who is seeking information about Dantès. Faced with the fact that he is destroying an innocent man's happiness for the sake of his own ambitions, Villefort is seized with agonizing regret.

Chapter 10: The Little Room in the Tuileries
Villefort rushes to Paris to tell King Louis XVIII of the schemes contained in the letter Dantès was carrying. He informs the king that there is a conspiracy afoot to bring Napoleon back to power.

Chapter 11: The Corsican Ogre
Villefort's warning has come too late. Napoleon has already landed in France and is marching on Paris. Nevertheless, Villefort wins the king's gratitude, as he is the only person who was able to uncover Napoleon's plot in advance.

Chapter 12: Father and Son
Noirtier visits Villefort. Villefort tells his father that the police are looking for a man who fits Noirtier's description in connection with the murder of a royalist general. While Villefort looks on, Noirtier shaves his beard and changes his clothes. As he leaves, he tells Villefort that Napoleon is advancing quickly and is again being hailed as emperor by a still-admiring public.

Chapter 13: The Hundred Days
Napoleon quickly recaptures all of France. Now that Bonapartism is no longer considered a crime, Monsieur Morrel approaches Villefort multiple times to intercede on Dantès's behalf, but he is always placated with promises. Danglars, unaware that Villefort has an intense personal interest in keeping Dantès locked away, fears that Dantès will be released and then will seek revenge. Danglars resigns from Morrel's service and moves to Madrid. Fernand comforts Mercédès and wins her gratitude, but has to leave to join Napoleon's army. In the meantime, Dantès's father dies of misery over his son's imprisonment. Morrel pays for the old man's funeral and settles the small debts he has incurred. After only one hundred days in power, Napoleon is deposed again, and Louis XVIII reassumes the throne.

Chapter 14: In the Dungeons
The inspector-general of prisons visits the Château d'If, where Dantès begs him for a fair trial. The inspector is moved by Dantès's pleas and promises to look into his case. When he examines the register, he sees that Villefort wrote that Dantès took an active part in Napoleon's return from Elba. The inspector decides that he cannot help Dantès.

ANALYSIS: CHAPTERS 6–14

Nineteenth-century France was divided by a deep political schism between revolutionary Bonapartists, who hoped to bring Napoleon and his liberal democratic ideas back to the French throne, and conservative royalists, who were committed to the old French royal family and their traditional rule. This divide plays an important role in the early chapters of *The Count of Monte Cristo*. Characters associated with the Bonapartist cause, such as Morrel, Dantès, the dead captain, and Noirtier, are portrayed in a sympathetic light, while the aristocratic royalists, such as Villefort and the Marquise de Saint-Méran, are cast in the roles of villains. This stark division between good Bonapartists and bad royalists is not surprising, since Dumas was a great admirer of Napoleon and had strong democratic leanings. His father had been a general in Napoleon's army, and Dumas grew up with a love of freedom and a respect for individual rights.

The Count of Monte Cristo is heavily tinged with these Napoleonic ideals, which Dumas clearly prefers over the old aristocratic tenets. Dantès is undone not only by the jealousy of dishonorable men but also by the oppressive political system of the post-revolutionary era, a system that routinely sentenced suspected radicals to life in prison with little or no proof of guilt. Dantès is a pawn in a game of political intrigue, and his rights as an individual are ignored as Villefort uses him to advance his personal political goals. Furthermore, Noirtier paints a bleak picture of modern political regimes when he tells his son that "in politics . . . there are no men, but ideas—no feelings, but interests; in politics we do not kill a man, we only remove an obstacle." The political system's prioritization of ideas over men and interests over feelings, along with its perception of man as an obstacle, is a natural outcome of its impersonal and dehumanizing nature. Like Napoleon himself, Dantès eventually emerges as a champion for the rights of the individual, working against the oppressive tyranny of the political system.

Dantès's lack of intellectual opinions follows a model of the Romantic ideal. Indeed, Dantès is a living embodiment of the Romantic idea of the cult of feelings. Romanticism, a cultural movement in nineteenth-century Europe, viewed emotion as superior to intellect and admired the human who feels over the human who calculates. Dantès simply loves and admires; he does not analyze or judge. Interestingly, when he emerges later as the Count of Monte

Cristo, he is guided only by ideas. He is specifically motivated by one idea—revenge; consequently, he becomes incapable of feeling normal human sentiments. Given Dumas's affiliation with the Romantic movement, it is not surprising to find that the Dantès of the early chapters, a man of unimpeachable character, is portrayed as a person dominated by emotion. For the same reason, it makes sense that when Dantès later falls into error and sin, becoming a strange mixture of hero and antihero, it is his intellect that takes over as a dominating yet dangerous force. This dichotomy between emotion and intellect allows Dumas to show his belief in the supremacy of the Romantic individual over the rational human being.

By giving Chapter 12 the same subtitle as Chapter 2—"Father and Son"—Dumas invites us to compare the two father-son pairs portrayed in these chapters. In Chapter 2 the father and son are Louis and Edmond Dantès, a pair bound by absolute love and devotion. In Chapter 12, however, the father-son pair of Noirtier and Villefort is bound by little more than mutual distrust. When Dantès hears of his newfound good fortune, his first thought is of how he might improve life for his father; he fantasizes about all the nice things his newfound affluence will enable him to provide for the old man. Villefort, in contrast, is prepared to sacrifice his father in order to increase his own fortune. Though Villefort warns his father that the authorities are searching for a man of his description, this act is motivated not by loyalty but by self-interest: Villefort knows that his own career will be ruined if his father is charged with murder. Later, Villefort attempts to break all ties with Noirtier, even going so far as to renounce his family name. When his future in-laws ask him to state his allegiances, Villefort has no qualms about harshly denouncing his father. Here, filial loyalty serves to underscore the vast difference in character between Dantès and Villefort. Dantès's devotion to his father reveals his kindness and basic goodness, while Villefort's neglect and betrayal of his father expose him as a heartless conniver, looking out only for himself.

CHAPTERS 15–20

CHAPTER 15: NUMBER 34 AND NUMBER 27

During his first six years in prison, Dantès initially turns to God, immersing himself in prayer. As he contemplates his bad luck, his despair increasingly turns to wrath. Dantès does not yet know that envious men are responsible for his unfortunate imprisonment. He is so sick with grief and hopelessness that he finally decides to kill himself by means of starvation. Just when he feels that he is about to die, however, he hears a scratching sound coming from the other side of his cell.

When the jailer comes to give him his dinner, Dantès cleverly places his dish in a spot where the jailer will be sure to step on it. The dish shatters and the jailer leaves the entire pot for Dantès. Dantès is thus able to use the handle of the pot to begin scraping at the wall from his side. After hours of scraping he hears the voice of his neighbor. Later, they break through, and his neighbor emerges through the hole in the wall.

CHAPTER 16: A LEARNED ITALIAN
Dantès's neighbor tells him that his name is Abbé Faria and that he has been imprisoned for his political beliefs, as he is an agitator for a unified Italy. Dantès realizes that Abbé Faria is the mad priest that the jailer once mentioned. Dantès is overjoyed to have a companion. The abbé is less happy to see Dantès, however, as he had mistakenly believed he had been digging a tunnel to freedom.

CHAPTER 17: IN THE ABBÉ'S CELL

> [I]t has installed a new passion in your heart—that of vengeance.
>
> (See QUOTATIONS, p. 90)

Faria, rather than being insane, proves to be a brilliant and resourceful man. He has managed to fashion paper, ink, pens, a knife, a needle, a lamp, and various other necessities while imprisoned, and has used these to write a political treatise and dig the fifty-foot tunnel that connects his cell to Dantès's. When Dantès tells Faria his life story, Faria quickly discerns that Dantès has been framed by Danglars and Fernand. Faria is aware of the connection between Villefort and Noirtier, so he is able to explain that part of the mystery. Stunned by the discovery, Dantès turns his thoughts toward revenge.

Over the course of the next two years, the well-educated abbé teaches Dantès everything he knows. Dantès has a wonderful memory and a quick mind, and he is able to advance quickly in the study of mathematics, philosophy, history, and several languages. Faria develops another plot to escape, and the two men plan meticulously. Days before they are going to put the plan into action, however, Faria suffers a fit. His right arm and leg become paralyzed, leaving him unable to attempt escape. Dantès declares that he will not leave either, swearing to remain with Faria so long as the old man lives.

Chapter 18: The Treasure

The next day, Faria begins to talk about a hidden treasure, and Dantès becomes worried, thinking that his friend is insane after all. Faria convinces Dantès that the treasure truly exists by telling him the story behind it. The treasure once belonged to the Spada family, the wealthiest family in Italy. In the fifteenth century, Caesar Spada hid the treasure on the uninhabited island of Monte Cristo, hoping to keep it out of the hands of a murderous, thieving pope. Due to a mishap, however, the location of the treasure remained a secret even from the family.

During his employment as the private secretary to the last living member of the Spada family, Faria stumbled onto the secret message, written in a mysterious ink. Faria explains that Spada left all he had to Faria, so the treasure actually belongs to him. Faria says that the treasure also belongs to Dantès, who has become his spiritual son over the course of the past two years. Faria shows Dantès the piece of paper that reveals the treasure's location.

Chapter 19: The Death of the Abbé

Faria forces Dantès to commit the directions to the treasure to memory. Several nights later, Faria has another attack and dies.

Chapter 20: The Cemetery of the Château d'If

Dantès is thrown into utter despair as he sits with his friend's shrouded corpse. Suddenly, however, he hits upon a brilliant escape plan. He cuts open the shroud, removes Faria's corpse to his own cell, and then sews himself inside the shroud. Later that night, when the guards come to bury the corpse, it is Dantès they remove. Dantès, believing that dead prisoners are buried in a nearby cemetery, plans to dig his way out with a knife. Minutes after he is carried out of the cell, he discovers he is mistaken. The guards tie a cannonball around his legs and cast him into the sea.

Analysis: Chapters 15–20

The title of Chapter 15, "Number 34 and Number 27," indicates yet another crime of society against the individual. As prisoners, Dantès and Faria are reduced to numbers and are no longer addressed by their names. The disposal of Dantès's name is the final affront to his rights as an individual; it amounts to a loss of his self. As an individual, Dantès is deemed worthless when Villefort sacrifices him for his own political ambitions; this denial of his worth is made official with the loss of even his own name. Abbé Faria, who is also known merely as a number, saves Dantès's life and sanity by giving him back his sense of self. Once again treated as a human being and engaged in reciprocal conversation, Dantès rises out of his depression and finds new intellectual pursuits for which to live. Faria is able to counteract the harm that oppressive society has wreaked on Dantès by treating him as a human being.

Abbé Faria represents the eighteenth-century philosopher archetype that was prominent in literature of Dumas's day and that would have been familiar to Dumas's contemporary audience. The philosopher is a well-educated, well-read man who believes strongly in the power of human reason and closely studies human nature and human societies. Like the other sympathetic characters of the novel, Faria is a great admirer of Napoleon and a firm believer in the inevitability of national and personal freedom. By thoroughly educating Dantès, Faria gives him the potential to reach the highest aspirations that his individual nature permits. This emphasis on maximizing human potential was an obsession shared by the Revolution-influenced Romantics and the more rational philosophers represented by Faria. The fact that Dumas casts a rational, intellectual man like Faria in one of the most sympathetic roles in the novel demonstrates that Dumas does not rigidly adhere to the scorn of intellectualism that was typical of the Romantic movement.

Faria's deduction about the truth behind Dantès's downfall is the first major turning point in Dantès's development, as it is in this moment that Dantès begins his transformation from a happy, innocent, and loving man into a vengeful and miserable one. That Dantès is unable to fathom his enemies' treachery himself indicates the extent of his initial innocence. When he enters the prison, he is a person without malice; it never occurs to him that people could act as cruelly and selfishly as his enemies have. When Faria reveals the true cause of Dantès's imprisonment, Dantès's blinding naïveté is destroyed. Faria immediately apologizes to Dantès for telling him the truth about his history, knowing that he has infected him with vengeance and thus irrevocably transformed him. Dantès initially does not understand why Faria is apologizing to him, for he is happy to finally have the truth revealed. However, he soon realizes the oppressive weight of his newfound knowledge. Coupled with the knowledge of an enormous treasure that may soon be his own, Dantès, much to his horror, finds himself thinking only of the amount of harm he could wreak with such a fortune instead of the pleasure it could bring him. Now aware of the evil deeds committed against him, he has become overwhelmed with the desire for vengeance and has thus lost his capacity to enjoy life with the innocence of his past.

Dumas compares Dantès's imprisonment to death, which casts Dantès's later actions and circumstances as a rebirth or resurrection. In Chapter 14, the narrator tells us that Dantès "looked upon himself as dead," while in Chapter 17, Dantès himself refers to prison as "a living grave." This morbid language signifies a metaphorical death: the happy, innocent Dantès of the early chapters dies and is replaced by the vengeful, bitter man of the remainder of the novel. This death is not merely one of innocence, but perhaps also one of humanity. The Dantès who emerges from prison is not simply vengeful: he is nearly superhuman in his mental and physical capabilities, while subhuman in his emotional capacity. He is something both greater and less than a human being.

CHAPTERS 21–25

CHAPTER 21: THE ISLE OF TIBOULEN

Dantès manages to cut himself loose from the shroud and swims in the direction of an uninhabited island he remembers from his sailing days. When he feels that he cannot swim any longer, he washes up on the jagged rocks of the island. A storm erupts, and Dantès watches helplessly as a small boat crashes against the rocks, killing all the men on board. He then sees a Genoese ship in the distance and realizes that this ship is his one chance to finalize his escape. He takes the cap of one of the dead sailors off the point of a rock and makes his way to the ship, using a piece of driftwood from the destroyed boat as a float. Dantès tells the men on the ship that he was the lone survivor among the sailors who crashed on the rocks during the storm. His long hair and beard arouse the men's suspicion, but Dantès passes his shagginess off as a religious pledge made to God in a time of danger. The men believe his story and offer to take him on as one of their crew.

CHAPTER 22: THE SMUGGLERS

Dantès quickly realizes that the men on the ship are smugglers, but he makes himself useful to them, and they all grow to love him. He patiently waits for a chance to land on the island of Monte Cristo.

This chance finally presents itself when the ship's captain decides to use the deserted island as the site for an illegal transaction.

CHAPTER 23: THE ISLE OF MONTE CRISTO
While on the island, Dantès pretends to injure himself and claims that he cannot be moved. He urges the men to leave him behind and return for him after a week. Dantès's best friend among the crew, Jacopo, offers to stay behind, forgoing his share of the profits from the smuggling operation. Dantès is moved by this selfless display, but refuses the offer.

CHAPTER 24: THE SEARCH
Once the men are gone, Dantès begins searching for Faria's treasure. He uses his enormous ingenuity to uncover the fortune, which is even greater than he had imagined. Dantès falls on his knees and utters a prayer to God, to whom he attributes this windfall.

CHAPTER 25: AT MARSEILLES AGAIN
Dantès fills his pockets with a few precious stones from his trove and waits for the sailors to return. He then sails with them to Leghorn, where he sells the four smallest diamonds for five thousand francs each. The following day, Dantès buys a small ship and crew for Jacopo in order to reward his friend's kindness. His one condition for the gift is that Jacopo sail to Marseilles and ask for news of a man named Louis Dantès and a woman named Mercédès.

Dantès takes his leave of the smugglers and buys a yacht with a secret compartment. He sails the yacht back to Monte Cristo and transfers the remainder of the treasure to the secret compartment of the yacht. Jacopo arrives on the island several days later with sad news: Louis Dantès is dead and Mercédès has disappeared. Dantès tries to hide his extreme emotion and sails for Marseilles.

ANALYSIS: CHAPTERS 21–25
Just as Dantès's imprisonment is portrayed as a sort of death, his escape is cast as a sort of rebirth. Dantès emerges into the free world by way of water, clearly a symbolic reference to the Christian tradition of baptism, in which a newborn baby is doused with water in order to dedicate its soul to God. Dantès is reborn as a man with a single mission—to avenge the wrongs done to him. His baptismal pledge, then, can be seen as a pledge to carry out this vengeance, which he believes is God's will. Signs of Dantès's transformation emerge immediately, as we see when he boards the smugglers' ship

bearing falsehoods about his identity. The Dantès of the early chapters is a compulsively honest man, yet he now lies easily and skillfully about his identity. His constructs his first lie without a second thought, and he follows with a barrage of other untruths. Dantès's radically different behavior indicates that he is a new man, born during his imprisonment and baptized during his watery escape.

Dumas challenges the rigid and judgmental expectations of French society in portraying the smugglers as good, even admirable men. The smugglers' actions have little to do with justice in an ethical sense. Indeed, though *The Count of Monte Cristo* is a novel about justice, the concept of justice in the novel is deep and complex, based on fundamental ethical rights rather than societal law. Indeed, Dantès's concept of justice does not at all match up with civil society's concept of justice. The distinction between Dantès's concept of justice and society's concept of justice is further underscored by the fact that the public prosecutor, Villefort—who, we see later, is portrayed as the human arbiter of societal law—is cast as a vile and unjust character. Dumas's message is clear: societal justice is really no justice at all, as it punishes moral and good people for petty crimes that have nothing to do with real justice, while rewarding the vile and unethical with wealth and power.

In Chapter 24, Dumas begins to explore an important difference between lives filled with hope and lives filled with hopelessness. Preparing himself for the disappointment of not finding the treasure, Dantès reflects that "[t]he heart breaks when, after having been elated by flattering hopes, it sees all these illusions destroyed." He thus acknowledges that hope is what keeps a human being going and that hopelessness is the only thing that destroys the human spirit. Dantès begins to understand that happiness and despair stem from expectations, not from what one actually has or does not have. With all his desires now pinned on enacting his revenge, Dantès realizes that he faces the possibility of falling into despair once again if he finds no treasure and thus cannot hope to carry out his revenge. He attempts to dim his hopes in order to save himself the crippling pain that would result if he finds these hopes thwarted.

When Dantès locates the treasure, he considers the event both "joyous and terrible," because he knows that with this wealth, he must now begin the obsessive, dark endeavor that will consume him for the next decade. He must sever ties to normal human life and devote himself to destroying his enemies. This daunting task is made possible by his fortune alone, and so the fortune itself frightens him.

Only when Dantès prays is he able to feel the day is at all "joyous." His prayer calms the feelings of horror and revulsion that the sight of his treasure stirs up and convinces him that God supports his mission of revenge. Dantès convinces himself that only God could have orchestrated the successful discovery of such an enormous treasure, and that the treasure exists for the very purpose of carrying out a terrible punishment on Dantès's enemies.

As we see later, Dantès's conviction that God is using him as an instrument to carry out divine will continues to buoy his determination throughout the novel. Given Dantès's religious interpretation of his mission, it is significant that the island where he finds his treasure is called "Monte Cristo," which in Italian means "the mountain of Christ." This religious conception of his mission and Dantès's certainty about its legitimacy allow him to overlook the "terrible" aspect of his discovery and bask in its "joyous" aspect.

CHAPTERS 26–30

CHAPTER 26: THE INN OF PONT DU GARD
Disguised as an Italian priest and going by the name of Abbé Busoni, Dantès travels to the inn owned by Caderousse and his sickly wife. He finds the couple poverty-stricken. Pretending to be the executor of Dantès's will, he explains that Dantès came into the possession of a large diamond while in prison. He adds that, as his dying wish, Dantès wanted the diamond's worth divided among the only five people he ever loved: his father, Caderousse, Danglars, Fernand, and Mercédès.

CHAPTER 27: THE TALE
Seeing his chance to secure the whole diamond for himself, Caderousse reveals the events behind Dantès's incarceration, confirming what Abbé Faria had already deduced. Caderousse states that he has lived in a torment of regret ever since Dantès was incarcerated. Dantès finds this display of repentance and guilt convincing, and he declares that Caderousse is Dantès's only true friend. He gives Caderousse the entire diamond.

Dantès learns from Caderousse what has become of the others. Danglars went to work for a Spanish banking house and ended up a millionaire; he is now one of the richest and most powerful men in Paris. Fernand has also become rich and powerful, though the circumstances of how he acquired his fortune are mysterious. Fernand returned wealthy from his tour of duty as a soldier in Greece and married Mercédès eighteen months after Dantès's imprisonment began. Fernand and Mercédès now live together in Paris, believing Dantès to be dead.

Caderousse also explains that Dantès's father, Louis, starved himself to death out of grief over the loss of his son. Both Morrel and Mercédès offered many times to take the old man into their homes and care for him, but he refused every time. Morrel tried to give Louis money, and before the old man's death, he left a red silk purse filled with gold on his mantel. Caderousse now has this red silk purse in his possession, and Dantès asks to have it. Caderousse explains that Morrel is now on the verge of financial ruin: all his ships except the *Pharaon* have sunk, and the *Pharaon* is late coming into port. If the *Pharaon* has sunk, Morrel will be unable to pay his creditors and will be a ruined man. Caderousse reflects that the good are always punished and the wicked rewarded. Dantès, in the guise of the priest, promises Caderousse that this is not the case.

Chapter 28: The Prison Registers

Next, disguised as an English representative of the investment firm Thomson and French, Dantès goes to visit the mayor of Marseilles, who has a large investment in Morrel's shipping business. The mayor redirects Dantès to the inspector of prisons, who has an even larger stake in Morrel's firm. Dantès buys all of the prison inspector's stakes for their full price. He then asks to see the prison records for Abbé Faria, claiming to have once been his pupil. While looking at the records, Dantès secretly turns to his own prison documents. He pockets the letter of accusation written by Danglars and delivered by Fernand, and confirms the fact that Villefort ordered him locked away for life.

Chapter 29: The House of Morrel and Son

Still disguised as the representative of Thomson and French, Dantès next pays a visit to Morrel. Morrel is in a state of extreme anxiety over the fact that his once bustling shipping firm is now crumbling into ruin. Only two employees remain on his payroll, including a twenty-three-year-old clerk, Emmanuel Herbaut, who is in love with Morrel's daughter, Julie. Morrel's payments to investors are due within days, but he has no money to cover them. If the *Pharaon* does not arrive safely, he will be unable to honor his debts for the first time in his life, and his business and his honor will be permanently ruined.

The terrible news arrives while Dantès is still in Morrel's office: the *Pharaon* has been lost. Dantès, who now owns a significant percentage of the debt Morrel owes, grants the devastated man a reprieve. He tells Morrel that he can have an extra three months to find the money to make the payment. On his way out of the building, Dantès pulls Julie aside and makes her promise to follow any instructions she receives from a man calling himself "Sinbad the Sailor."

CHAPTER 30: THE FIFTH OF SEPTEMBER

The three months draw to a close, and Morrel still has very little money. He decides that he must take his own life, unable to bear the shame of breaking his obligation to creditors. On the day that his debt is due, Morrel confides his plan to his son, Maximilian, and his son understands, granting his approval. As Morrel and Maximilian share this morbid discussion, Julie receives a letter from Sinbad the Sailor. She follows the instructions in the letter and finds the red silk purse her father once gave to Louis Dantès. It is filled with Morrel's debt notes, which are marked as paid. The purse also contains a tremendous diamond tagged for use as Julie's dowry, enabling her to marry Emmanuel.

Julie bursts in with this miraculous find just as her father cocks his gun to take his own life. They hear an uproar from outside. A ship built and painted to look exactly like the *Pharaon* is pulling into the port, laden with the same cargo that the original had been carrying when it was lost at sea. Amid this happy scene, Dantès boards his yacht and departs Marseilles.

ANALYSIS: CHAPTERS 26–30

Dantès's speech in these chapters makes it clear that he truly considers himself an agent of Providence rather than a man merely carrying out a good cause. He feels qualified to tell Caderousse that "God may seem sometimes to forget for a while, whilst his justice reposes, but there always comes a moment when he remembers." Here, Dantès implies that the signal that God "remembers," in this particular case, is that God has given him this vast fortune to use as a tool of reward and punishment. As Dantès departs Marseilles, he reflects, "I have been Heaven's substitute to recompense the good—now the God of Vengeance yields to me his power to punish the wicked!" In calling himself "Heaven's substitute," Dantès could not be more explicit about how he views his role. Given that he clearly considers himself God's emissary on earth, it is fitting that he chooses to disguise himself as a priest when visiting Caderousse. In some traditions, the priest acts as a direct intermediary between God and man—the same role Dantès sees himself as occupying in his quest for revenge.

Each of Dantès's various disguises correlates with the role that he plays while assuming that identity. He tends to dress as the Abbé Busoni when he is standing in judgment; thus, he dons the Abbé Busoni disguise when visiting Caderousse, as he must decide whether Caderousse should be rewarded as a friend or punished as an enemy. When engaging in acts of excessive generosity, as he does toward Morrel, Dantès dresses as an Englishman whom we later learn he refers to as Lord Wilmore. Dantès tends to use the name Sinbad the Sailor when acting in a particularly eccentric manner, though he primarily makes use of this name when in Italy. Later, Dantès assumes the name Monte Cristo when acting as an angel of vengeance. Like the God of the Old Testament, who uses a different name to refer to each of his different aspects—his punishing side and his compassionate side, for example—Dantès, a self-appointed emissary of God on earth, also fractures his personality into its various components: judging, rewarding, and punishing. Like God, he assigns each aspect a different identity.

Of all the names Dantès uses, Sinbad the Sailor bears its own original significance, as it is a recognizable name. Sinbad the Sailor is a character in a famous Middle Eastern folktale about a merchant who goes on seven dangerous and fantastical journeys, ultimately ending up enormously wealthy. There are many reasons why Dantès might have chosen this familiar name as one of his aliases. There is the obvious fact that Dantès himself was a sailor during the happy years of his life. Likewise, there is a clear parallel between Sinbad's seven dangerous voyages leading up to his ultimate wealth and Dantès's own dangerous journey through prison before the discovery of his treasure.

Another, and more meaningful, possible explanation for this name involves the bookends of the Sinbad story, which focus on a poor porter who envies Sinbad's wealth and is dissatisfied with his own boring life. By the end of Sinbad's story, which is filled with horrors and dangers, the porter is convinced his own life is not so bad after all. This change in attitude highlights a central idea in *The Count of Monte Cristo* that becomes increasingly important as the novel unfolds: the importance of appreciating what one has in life instead of lusting after what one does not have. Each of Dantès's three enemies betrays him out of greed and ambition, giving in to lust for what he does not have. Danglars betrays Dantès to win the captaincy of the *Pharaon*, Fernand betrays Dantès to gain Mercédès for himself, and Villefort betrays Dantès to increase his own power. By using the name Sinbad the Sailor, Dantès tacitly rebukes these three men for their shortsighted greed.

The red silk purse, which holds Dantès's gift to Morrel, serves as a physical symbol of the connection between good deed and reward. First used by Morrel to help save Louis Dantès, the purse is now used to save Morrel in turn, demonstrating that his kindness and generosity toward Louis are being repaid. However, Dantès's use of the purse actually taints an otherwise pure act of altruism. By using the purse, Dantès reveals that on some level he *wants* Morrel to recognize him as the savior. We see the purse not merely as a simple symbol of the connection between reward and punishment but as a more complex embodiment of Dantès's various motives in acting as a benefactor. Dantès has selfless gratitude for Morrel's kindness but also a selfish desire to be recognized as the author of Morrel's financial salvation.

CHAPTERS 31–34

CHAPTER 31: ITALY: SINBAD THE SAILOR

Ten years after the events in Marseilles, an aristocratic young Parisian named Baron Franz d'Epinay makes a stop on the island of Monte Cristo to hunt wild goats, at the suggestion of his Italian guides. Franz finds a band of men on the island whom he takes to be a group of smugglers. He later learns that they are the crew of a yacht belonging to a fabulously wealthy man who is rumored to travel constantly. The man goes by the name Sinbad the Sailor.

Franz is brought to meet Sinbad at his fabulous palace, which is hidden inside the rocks. He is stunned by the Oriental luxury of the man, his abode, and the food he offers. Sinbad—who is, of course, Dantès—tells Franz that he travels all over the world performing eccentric acts of philanthropy, such as saving bandits from punishment. Sinbad explains, for instance, how he met his mute Nubian slave, Ali. Found wandering too near the king's harem in Tunis, Ali was sentenced to have his tongue and hand cut off, followed by his head. Hearing of this decree and wanting a mute slave, Sinbad waited until Ali's tongue was cut out, then bought his freedom. Sinbad then rhapsodizes on the wonders of hallucinogenic drugs, in which he and Franz subsequently both indulge. Franz experiences a vivid drug-induced fantasy.

CHAPTER 32: THE AWAKENING

The next morning, Franz tries for hours to find the opening to Sinbad's hidden grotto, but is unsuccessful. After giving up the search, he travels to Rome to meet Viscount Albert de Morcerf, the son of Fernand Mondego, who is now known as the Count de Morcerf. The two friends are planning to stay in the city for the duration of the citywide carnival that precedes Lent. Arriving late and unprepared, they find themselves unable to rent a coach, which is necessary for enjoying the carnival.

CHAPTER 33: ROMAN BANDITS

The hotel owner warns Franz and Albert of the danger of bandits, especially the notorious Luigi Vampa. Finding his guests somewhat skeptical that such a threat really exists, he launches into the story of Vampa's rise to fame. Vampa was a young shepherd with a quick mind and a love for learning, sculpting, shooting, and a beautiful young shepherdess named Teresa. One day, the famous bandit leader Cucumetto stumbled upon Vampa and Teresa while fleeing the authorities. The couple hid Cucumetto, even though a large reward had been offered for his capture.

CHAPTER 34: VAMPA

The hotel owner continues Vampa's story: at a splendid party, the frivolous Teresa danced with a nobleman and lusted after the ornate costume of the aristocratic hostess. Vampa, overcome with envy and the desire to keep Teresa for himself, promised that he would get the costume for her. That night he set the host's house on fire, seizing the costume in the ensuing panic. The following day, as Teresa changed into her costume, Vampa gave directions to a lost traveler named Sinbad the Sailor, who in return gave Vampa two small jewels. When Vampa came back from directing Sinbad the Sailor, he saw that Teresa was being kidnapped. He killed the assailant, realizing only afterward that it was Cucumetto. Vampa dressed himself in Cucumetto's clothes, approached the remaining bandits, and demanded to be made their new leader.

ANALYSIS: CHAPTERS 31–34

In the ten years that intervene between the events in Marseilles and the meeting between Franz and Dantès, Dantès's rebirth as the mysterious Count of Monte Cristo is complete. We have as little knowledge of the events of this intervening decade as any character in the story, and these lost years provide Monte Cristo with the requisite air of mystery. We are given only tantalizing hints of his life during this period, but enough to know that he has seen and experienced almost everything the world has to offer. Dantès emerges from these ten mysterious years as an almost supernatural being: he comes across as omniscient and omnipotent, possesses seemingly all possible human knowledge and superhuman physical strength, and maintains a level of cunning that gives him a nearly magical aura. Even Dantès's appearance is supernatural, sometimes compared to that of a corpse and other times to that of a vampire. His flesh too is described as oddly inhuman, causing Franz to shudder when he touches it. The transformation that begins in prison has now been carried so far that the Monte Cristo we find in Chapter 31 (though he calls himself Sinbad) bears virtually no resemblance to the Dantès we leave in Chapter 30.

Monte Cristo is an odd juxtaposition of intriguing characteristics. He lives a lifestyle that seems to be aimed at maximizing pleasure: he surrounds himself with excellent food, beautiful women, drugs, and every imaginable physical luxury. Yet Monte Cristo does not actually appear to enjoy the pleasures that surround him. He barely eats any of the food he has prepared and hints that he does not touch the lovely women in his service. All of his thoughts, instead, are occupied by pain, death, and revenge. Hallucinogenic drugs are the only luxury in which he indulges, since they allow him to escape his all-encompassing obsession for short periods of time. Part of the reason Monte Cristo surrounds himself with luxury is simply to impress other people. Indeed, all who meet him are dazzled by his ability to insinuate himself into any situation and carry out his plan of vengeance. Dumas may also have intended his depiction of Monte Cristo's sumptuous lifestyle merely as a treat for his nineteenth-century audience, which had a taste for books about the exotic.

Monte Cristo's fascination with and idealization of hallucinogenic drugs is typical of the Romantic mind-set. The Romantic interest in drugs is connected to the idea of the cult of feelings, the notion that feeling provides a superior means of accessing the world than intellect does. Since hallucinogenic drugs provide experiences that would not otherwise be possible—strange visions, new sensations, and novel experiences of the familiar—Romantic writers believed that these drugs could deepen their understanding of the world and could perhaps even improve their emotional and sentient lives.

The Romantic interest in drugs was also connected to the Romantic obsession with moving beyond human limits, an obsession the Romantic poet Percy Bysshe Shelley described as "the desire of the moth for a star." Dumas emphasizes this connection between drugs and human transcendence when he has Dantès declare that drugs cause "the boundaries of possibility [to] disappear." The boundaries of which Dantès speaks refer to the human limitations that the Romantic writers strove to exceed—or, at least, that they had their characters strive to exceed. According to Dantès, drugs allow one to move beyond human limits by providing a form of experience in which these limits do not exist. Dantès's eloquent speech in honor of hallucinogenic drugs and the drug-induced reverie that follows reveals Dumas's accepting attitude toward this typical Romantic fascination.

CHAPTERS 35–39

CHAPTER 35: THE COLOSSEUM
While visiting the Colosseum in Rome, Franz overhears a conversation between his mysterious Monte Cristo host (Dantès) and the bandit chief Luigi Vampa. An innocent shepherd named Peppino has been arrested for being an accomplice to bandits. Although he merely provided them with food, he has been sentenced to a public beheading, which is to take place in two days. Monte Cristo promises to buy Peppino's freedom, and Vampa pledges his everlasting loyalty in return.

The next evening, Franz and Albert attend the opera, and Franz again sees his mysterious host. Monte Cristo is accompanied by Haydée, the most beautiful woman Franz has ever seen, dressed in a Greek costume. The lovely Countess G—, who is sitting with Franz and Albert, is terrified by the mysterious and deathly pale Monte Cristo, whom she is certain is a vampire. The following morning, the hotel owner informs Franz and Albert that their fellow guest, Monte Cristo, has offered to lend them his coach for the duration of the carnival. Albert and Franz pay a visit to Monte Cristo, and Franz is stunned to discover that he is the same man who acted as his mysterious host on the island of Monte Cristo.

CHAPTER 36: LA MAZZOLATA

Before breakfast, Monte Cristo invites the two young men to watch a public execution from his private windows. He admits to a fascination with executions. The three men engage in a discussion about the limits and shortcomings of human justice. At the execution, one of the two condemned, Peppino, is granted a reprieve. Monte Cristo watches impassively as the other is brutally executed. He appears to take great pleasure in watching vengeance play out.

CHAPTER 37: THE CARNIVAL AT ROME

During the three days of the carnival, Albert becomes engaged in an elaborate flirtation with a beautiful woman. He is eager to have several love affairs while in Rome and decides to devote all his energies to pursuing this opportunity.

CHAPTER 38: THE CATACOMBS OF SAINT SEBASTIAN

The beautiful woman turns out to be Luigi Vampa's mistress, Teresa, and the flirtation is actually a trap. The bandit chief kidnaps Albert, and Franz receives a ransom note. Unable to pay the ransom, he approaches Monte Cristo for help. Peppino, who delivered the ransom note, leads Franz and Monte Cristo to the bandits' lair in the Catacombs of Saint Sebastian. Vampa greets Monte Cristo warmly and sets Albert free with many apologies. Though Albert is surprisingly unfazed by the fact that he has so narrowly escaped a grisly end, he is nonetheless enormously grateful to Monte Cristo for saving him.

CHAPTER 39: THE RENDEZVOUS

In return for saving his life, Monte Cristo asks Albert to introduce him to Parisian society when he visits the city in three months' time. Albert is delighted. Franz, however, is wary, noting that Monte Cristo seems to shudder involuntarily when he is forced to shake hands with Albert. In an attempt to warn his friend away from Monte Cristo, Franz tells Albert about his experience on the isle of Monte Cristo and the conversation between Vampa and Monte Cristo he overheard in the Colosseum. This additional information leaves Albert only more enchanted with his savior.

ANALYSIS: CHAPTERS 35–39

Dumas was well known as a travel writer and dramatist before he became popular as a novelist, and we can see his talent for travel writing in this section of the novel. Travel writing was a very popular form of entertainment in the nineteenth century, and exotic locations were a particular public obsession. Generally, anywhere south of the country in which one resided counted as exotic; so, to French audiences, Italy certainly qualified. Dumas's vibrant portrait of Italy depicts a place that is alluringly colorful, sensual, exciting—and, perhaps most important, different from France.

Italy, as Dumas describes it, is full of spectacles, including the execution and the carnival. In some respects, such as its gruesome public executions, Italy is portrayed as more primitive than other civilizations to the north. In other respects, such as the stylish and urbane behavior of its women, Italy is portrayed as more sophisticated than these northern countries. In addition to Italy, Dumas also taps into the French obsession with Greece by introducing the character of Haydée. Greece was of particular interest to French writers of Dumas's era because of the Greek struggle for independence from Great Britain in the 1820s. By setting scenes of his novel in Greece, Italy, Constantinople, and even Marseilles—a city in the southernmost part of France—Dumas put his talent for travel writing to work and satisfied the public demand for exciting descriptions of exotic places.

Countess G—'s suspicion that Monte Cristo is a vampire connects the novel to yet another staple of Romanticism: a fascination with horror stories in general and vampires in particular. Countess G— repeatedly calls Monte Cristo by the name "Lord Ruthven," referring to the main character in a popular 1816 story entitled "The Vampyre." Though "The Vampyre" was actually written by Dr. John William Polidari, it was widely misattributed to the famous Romantic poet Lord Byron, which gave it enormous popularity. Charles Nodier wrote a drama based on the saga of Lord Ruthven, and Dumas wrote another Lord Ruthven play soon thereafter. The Romantic interest in vampires continued throughout the nineteenth century, culminating in the publication of Bram Stoker's *Dracula* in 1897. Lord Ruthven was considered both terrifying and alluring, two traits Monte Cristo clearly embodies as well. In a later chapter, the character Lucien Debray gives a description of a vampire that, according to Albert, describes Monte Cristo precisely. Like a vampire, Monte Cristo is a man partly of this world and partly of another world, simultaneously appealing and terrifying.

The breakfast discussion among Monte Cristo, Franz, and Albert raises several interesting issues about the limits of human justice. Monte Cristo explains that his dissatisfaction with human justice stems not only from the fact that the system sometimes allows the guilty to fall through the cracks, going unpunished for heinous crimes, but also from the fact that modern means of punishment are insufficient. The worst punishment that the modern criminal justice system will impose is death, yet death is nothing compared to the agony that many victims of crime suffer. Monte Cristo wonders whether it is enough that a criminal "who has caused us years of moral sufferings undergoes a few moments of physical pain." Monte Cristo's remarks offer a deep psychological insight into his mind as an avenger. He cannot feel any satisfaction until his enemies undergo something as painful as that which they have inflicted upon him. We can surmise from Monte Cristo's words that the revenge scheme he is planning is no simple murder plot—like the plot hatched by Piçaud, the real life model for Monte Cristo—but rather an attempt to destroy his enemies psychologically and emotionally.

Here, Dumas portrays Albert as a frivolous child who naïvely courts danger and adventure. When he first hears of the existence of the notorious Luigi Vampa, he wants to take off immediately to fight the bandit chief. Albert is also desperate to have numerous romantic adventures while in Italy. His silliness, though, is presented as a natural aspect of his youth, not an essential defect of character. In fact, Albert's uninquiring gratitude toward Monte Cristo and his bravery in Vampa's lair demonstrate that he has the makings of a noble adult. Aside from Monte Cristo, Albert is one of the few characters in the novel to undergo psychological development as the story progresses.

CHAPTERS 40–46

CHAPTER 40: THE GUESTS
On the day that Monte Cristo is supposed to arrive at Albert's house, Albert invites several friends for breakfast. Among those eagerly awaiting Monte Cristo's arrival are Lucien Debray, the secretary to the minister of the interior, and Beauchamp, a journalist.

CHAPTER 41: THE BREAKFAST
Two more guests arrive: the Baron of Château-Renaud, a diplomat, and Maximilian Morrel, who is now a captain in the French army. We learn that Maximilian once saved Château-Renaud's life in Constantinople, on the anniversary of the day Maximilian's father was miraculously saved from ruin, a day Maximilian always observes by trying to accomplish some heroic act.

Monte Cristo arrives in Paris and travels straight to Albert's house. Monte Cristo enchants all the guests, but he alone seems taken with Maximilian. Monte Cristo regales everyone with the story of how he once captured Luigi Vampa and his bandits and then let them go on the condition that they never harm either himself or his friends.

CHAPTER 42: THE PRESENTATION
When the guests have left, Albert shows Monte Cristo around his house. Monte Cristo exhibits a deep knowledge of all subjects scientific, humanistic, and artistic. Albert shows Monte Cristo a portrait of his mother, painted in the costume of a Catalan fisherwoman and looking mournfully out at the sea. He explains that he keeps the portrait in his house because his father hates it.

Albert then presents Monte Cristo to his mother and father. Fernand, who is now a senator, does not recognize Monte Cristo as Dantès and is easily charmed by him. Mercédès recognizes Dantès instantly, and she is terrified. She vaguely warns Albert to beware of his new friend.

CHAPTER 43: MONSIEUR BERTUCCIO
After taking leave of the Morcerf family, Monte Cristo purchases a summerhouse in Auteuil. The previous owner was the Marquis of Saint-Méran, whose daughter married Villefort and died soon after.

CHAPTER 44: THE HOUSE AT AUTEUIL
Monte Cristo goes to visit his new summerhouse. While he explores the grounds, his steward, Bertuccio, becomes frantic. When Monte Cristo presses him for an explanation of his agitation, Bertuccio unfolds a complex story.

CHAPTER 45: THE VENDETTA
Bertuccio explains that years ago, his brother, who had been a soldier in Napoleon's army, was murdered by royalist assassins in the city of Nîmes. Seeking justice, Bertuccio visited the public prosecutor of Nîmes, who at the time was Gérard de Villefort. Villefort, a royalist, was unsympathetic to Bertuccio's story and coolly turned him away. Bertuccio swore revenge on the public prosecutor.

Terrified for his life, Villefort transferred to Versailles, but Bertuccio followed him there. Bertuccio soon discovered that Villefort often came to visit the summerhouse in Auteuil, where he kept his mistress, a widowed baroness. One night, Bertuccio lay in wait for Villefort in the small garden behind the house and stabbed him, leaving him for dead. Villefort had just finished burying a box when Bertuccio pounced on him and grabbed the box, thinking that it contained a treasure. Instead, he found a baby, which had been smothered but started breathing after being given mouth-to-mouth resuscitation. Following a seven- or eight-month stay in the hospital, Bertuccio took the baby home with him and raised it with the help of his widowed sister-in-law.

The baby, whom Bertuccio and his sister-in-law named Benedetto, almost immediately showed signs of cruelty. As an older boy, he disappeared and was never heard from again. In the meantime, Bertuccio was away smuggling goods into France. On the run from the authorities, he ducked into a loft behind Caderousse's inn. While hiding in the loft behind Caderousse's inn, Bertuccio watched a terrible scene unfold. Caderousse and his wife had invited a jeweler to buy the diamond that the Abbé Busoni had just given them. After handing over forty-five thousand francs, the jeweler planned to return home, but a storm convinced him to spend the night at the inn.

CHAPTER 46: THE RAIN OF BLOOD
Bertuccio continues his story: seizing the chance to double his profit, Caderousse murdered both the jeweler and his own wife, then fled with the money and the diamond.

Arriving at the scene, the police arrested Bertuccio for the crime. Bertuccio remembered that Caderousse claimed to have received the diamond from a man named Abbé Busoni, so the authorities put out a search for the priest in order to clear Bertuccio of the crime. When Busoni turned up, he visited Bertuccio in prison. Bertuccio told the abbé his entire story, and Busoni suggested that should Bertuccio ever get out of prison, he should contact the Count of Monte Cristo, who would hire him as a steward. Soon thereafter, Caderousse turned up and confessed to the crime. Bertuccio was released and went to work for the Count of Monte Cristo, while Caderousse was sentenced to a lifetime of hard labor. Then, at the age of eleven, while Bertuccio was away on business, Benedetto tortured his adopted mother for a small amount of money and ended up killing her.

ANALYSIS: CHAPTERS 40–46
Dumas's roots as a playwright are apparent throughout *The Count of Monte Cristo,* perhaps most obviously in this section. Rather than merely present Bertuccio's history through a narrator, Dumas gives Bertuccio a long monologue. This monologue gives Bertuccio

the opportunity to reveal all that we need to know about his life and his connection to other major characters, namely Villefort and Caderousse. The context of the monologue is, admittedly, very forced: we know that Monte Cristo and Abbé Busoni are the same person, so we are aware that Monte Cristo already knows all the information he is forcing Bertuccio to reveal. The fact that Dumas resorts to such an awkward setup demonstrates the strength of his commitment to tell the story through dialogue. In fact, there is hardly a plot development or piece of internal history in the entire novel that does not unfold through dialogue. It is by means of the dialogue over breakfast in Chapters 40 and 41, for instance, that we learn about Maximilian's bravery and Monte Cristo's true connection to Luigi Vampa. Likewise, it is during the course of the conversation between Albert and Mercédès that we learn that Mercédès does in fact recognize Monte Cristo as Dantès. This heavy reliance on dialogue makes Dumas's novels seem like an extension of his dramatic work.

The unexpected appearance of Maximilian Morrel at Albert's house in Chapter 40 is a crucial plot twist. This twist prevents *The Count of Monte Cristo* from being merely a catalogue of rewards straightforwardly followed by punishments. For ten years Monte Cristo has been preparing himself to feel and act upon nothing but hatred and vengeance. The appearance of Maximilian calls up a set of different emotions for which Monte Cristo is not prepared. He is suddenly filled with gratitude and warmth—two sentiments that he has prepared to leave behind. Maximilian's presence complicates Monte Cristo's attempts to divide his life neatly into years devoted to rewarding and years spent punishing. As we later see, all such contact with the Morrel family throws Monte Cristo into uncertainty and discomfort. By inserting the Morrel family into this portion of the novel, Dumas forces Monte Cristo to grapple with unforeseen difficulty, which makes the story line more interesting.

The portrait of Mercédès looking mournfully out to sea hints that she has never forgotten, or ceased to love, Dantès. Her costume, that of a Catalan fisherwoman, symbolically connects Mercédès to Dantès, who was a sailor during the period when the two were engaged. As we learn in a later chapter, Mercédès has spent years under the mistaken impression that Dantès died at sea when he was thrown from the rocks in Abbé Faria's shroud. In her sad gaze toward the sea, then, she is focused on what she believes to be Dantès's grave. Even Fernand is obviously aware that the portrait signifies Mercédès's enduring feelings for Dantès, since he has it banished from his house. Mercédès's ability to recognize Dantès even through the changes of time and hardship also indicates the depth of her feeling for him. She has remained so thoroughly connected to him in her thoughts that she is immediately able to see through his new exterior. Mercédès's ability to recognize Dantès confirms what the portrait suggests: despite her marriage to Fernand, she has always remained loyal to Dantès in her heart.

CHAPTERS 47–53

CHAPTER 47: UNLIMITED CREDIT

Monte Cristo now engages in a clever, complex ruse to win the good graces of the Danglars and Villefort families. He instructs Bertuccio to purchase Danglars's two most beautiful horses for twice their asking price, knowing that these horses actually belong to Madame Danglars. With these two horses attached to his coach, Monte Cristo then visits Danglars at home in order to open an unlimited credit account with him, an act that astonishes and humbles Danglars.

CHAPTER 48: THE DAPPER GRAYS

While Monte Cristo is still at the Danglars residence, Madame Danglars is told that her horses have been sold, and she sees them attached to Monte Cristo's carriage. She becomes enraged with her husband for selling them. Monte Cristo excuses himself from the scene, as does Madame Danglars's lover, Lucien Debray. Later that evening, Monte Cristo, in a gallant gesture, returns the horses as a gift.

Knowing that Madame de Villefort will be borrowing these horses the next day, Monte Cristo arranges for the horses to become wild while they pass by his house. As the runaway horses go by, bearing the panic-stricken Madame de Villefort and her son, Edward, Ali, Monte Cristo's servant, lassos them easily, saving mother and son. Edward passes out from fear, and Monte Cristo uses a special potent elixir to revive him.

CHAPTER 49: IDEOLOGY

> *I wish to be Providence myself, for I feel that the most beautiful, noblest, most sublime thing in the world, is to recompense and punish.*
> (See QUOTATIONS, p. 91)

Villefort visits Monte Cristo in order to thank him for saving his wife and son. Monte Cristo engages Villefort in a conversation in which they compare civilized criminal justice systems to natural justice. Villefort reveals that his father, Noirtier, once one of the most powerful Jacobins and senators in France, has been paralyzed by a stroke.

CHAPTER 50: HAYDÉE

Monte Cristo goes to visit his beautiful Greek slave, Haydée, in her separate apartments, which are decorated in the most sumptuous Oriental style. He tells Haydée that she is free to do whatever she pleases and is free to leave him or stay with him. She pledges Monte Cristo her undying loyalty, but he reminds her that she is still only a child, twenty years old, and has the right to go off and live her own life whenever she chooses. The only thing Monte Cristo asks of Haydée is that she not reveal the "secret of her birth" to anyone in Paris.

CHAPTER 51: THE MORREL FAMILY

Monte Cristo pays a visit to Maximilian Morrel, who is staying with his sister, Julie. Julie is now married to Emmanuel Herbaut, the young clerk who remains loyal to Julie's father out of love for her. Their house is filled with a sense of bliss, love, and serenity that overwhelms Monte Cristo with emotion. When he comments on the uncommon happiness of this household, Emmanuel and Julie tell him of the angelic benefactor who once saved them. They show Monte Cristo the relics of this angel—the red silk purse and the diamond—and lament that they have never identified their benefactor.

Monte Cristo hazards a guess that the benefactor might have been an Englishman he once knew, a man named Lord Wilmore, who did not believe in true gratitude but performed many generous actions. Maximilian admits that his father has a more superstitious theory regarding their savior: he believes that their benefactor was Edmond Dantès, acting from beyond the grave. Monte Cristo is overwhelmed by this news, and he takes his leave abruptly and awkwardly.

CHAPTER 52: PYRAMUS AND THISBE

At the gate of Villefort's garden, Maximilian meets his secret love, Valentine de Villefort—Villefort's daughter from his first marriage. Valentine laments her sad fate: her father neglects her, her stepmother despises her, and she has a fiancé she does not want to marry. Maximilian makes Valentine promise not to resign herself to marrying Franz d'Epinay, despite her father's strong desire to see the union take place. As the two discuss their seemingly impossible

hope to be together—Maximilian is far too poor to be an appropriate match for Valentine and Villefort seems to hate the entire Morrel
family—the Count of Monte Cristo arrives at the Villefort home,
and Valentine is called away.

CHAPTER 53: TOXICOLOGY

Monte Cristo reminds Madame de Villefort that they have met once
before, in Italy. She recalls the meeting and is struck by the fact that
in Italy, Monte Cristo had been hailed as a great doctor because
he had saved two lives. Madame de Villefort expresses interest in
Monte Cristo's knowledge of chemistry, particularly his knowledge
of poisons. He describes to her the method he used to make himself
immune to poison and also describes an excellent antispasmodic
potion he has, which, as Madame de Villefort saw when Monte
Cristo revived Edward, is effective in small doses. Monte Cristo's
potion is lethal in large doses, however, but kills the victim in such
a way that he or she appears to die of natural causes. In response to
Madame de Villefort's hints, Monte Cristo offers to send her a vial
of the potion the next day.

ANALYSIS: CHAPTERS 47–53

When Villefort is reintroduced in Chapter 49, he is portrayed as a
rigid and inflexible "statue of the law," exacting a form of justice
that, according to Monte Cristo, is really no justice at all. Villefort
is obsessed with laws and rules, and he lives for the prosecution of
criminals. He cares little for human beings or for anything humanistic, such as art or entertainment; indeed, he is known as the "least
curious man in Paris." In Villefort we find an embodiment of all
that is wrong with the state of societal justice at Dumas's time. First,
Villefort's merciless application of the law parallels modern society's
own mercilessness to its citizens—particularly its poor citizens. In
addition, Villefort is hypocritical, brazenly breaking the very laws
he upholds, first by sentencing an innocent man to prison and then
by attempting to kill his own newborn son. Villefort's hypocrisy also
has a strong parallel in modern society, which rewards immorality
on the part of the wealthy and powerful. Danglars, for instance, is
rewarded generously for his financial opportunism. According to
Monte Cristo, modern societies are only thinly disguised tyrannies,
oppressing the common man and refusing him his rights as an individual and his equal protection under the law. Villefort, then, is the
living embodiment of—as well as the agent of—this tyranny.

The introduction of Haydée as a model of sumptuous, sensual Orientalism highlights Dumas's Romantic perspective and contrasts sharply with the rigidity of other characters such as Villefort and Danglars. Haydée's apartments, filled with silk cushions and diaphanous curtains, are decorated like something out of the collection of Eastern folktales known as *The Arabian Nights*. Haydée herself always dresses in her native Greek style, and even the food she eats is Oriental. The Romantic obsession with the exotic particularly favored such trappings of the Orient, a region considered incomparably mysterious. Romantics considered the women of the Orient far more desirable than European women, as well as more easily available. We see this Romantic notion of Oriental women in Dumas's description of Haydée as reclining on the ground in a position that "though perfectly natural for an Eastern female, would have been deemed too full of coquettish straining after effect in a European." The fact that Haydée can seem "perfectly natural" in a pose that would appear "strained" in a European emphasizes the degree to which the Romantics considered Oriental women more naturally alluring and sensual than European women. In addition, Haydée's exotic nature rubs off on Monte Cristo, bolstering his own mystique. Not only does Monte Cristo boast Haydée as a member of his household, but his grotto on the island of Monte Cristo is decorated in Oriental style, and he often claims to consider himself more Oriental than Western. Indeed, most of Monte Cristo's odd customs stem from the Orient. Haydée, with her dazzlingly unfamiliar beauty and her foreign way of life, typifies this Romantic notion of the exotic.

Chapters 50 and 51 demonstrate how perverse and almost inhuman Monte Cristo's psychology has become. Positive emotions, rather than vengeance and hatred, rattle him in the way that negative emotions would rattle most people. For Monte Cristo, the possibility of good feelings bothers him most. Faced with the prospect of visiting the Morrel family, an experience he knows will be fraught with good feeling, he prepares himself by visiting Haydée. He reflects that he "require[s] a gradual succession of calm and gentle emotions to prepare his mind to receive full and perfect happiness, in the same manner as ordinary natures demand to be inured by degrees to the reception of strong or violent sensations." This statement explicitly contrasts normal human psychology with Monte Cristo's perverse emotional life. Indeed, just as Monte Cristo has predicted, when he is with the Morrels his perfect, almost frightening composure deserts him for the first time. Confronted with the depth of the Morrels' gratitude, he becomes "pale as death, pressing one hand to his heart to still its throbbings." In the face of true goodness, Monte Cristo experiences the strong physical reaction that most people experience upon encountering something particularly gruesome or dark. His obsession with vengeance has completely perverted his nature.

The Morrel family has an enormous influence on Monte Cristo's estimation of humanity as a whole. Prior to meeting the Morrels, Monte Cristo believes that no human being is capable of feeling pure and true gratitude. He pessimistically announces to Franz and Albert that "man is an ungrateful and egotistical animal," then disdainfully remarks to Peppino, whose life he has saved, "you have not then forgotten that I saved your life; that is strange, for it is a week ago." Seeing the sincere and heartfelt thankfulness of the Morrels, however, Monte Cristo admits that Lord Wilmore would appreciate this gratitude and be "reconciled to mankind." Lord Wilmore is, of course, just another of Monte Cristo's aliases, and this statement is really an admission of Monte Cristo's own change of heart. It is Monte Cristo who is "reconciled to mankind" after he sees the Morrels provide such incontrovertible proof of humankind's capacity for gratitude.

Equally moving to Monte Cristo is the Morrels' complete satisfaction with their lives. Though hardly wealthy, they consider themselves enormously rich and choose not to pursue any further wealth, as they know that doing so would require them to be apart more often. Monte Cristo is shocked to see people so perfectly content in their daily existence, and he takes the Morrels as proof that happiness is determined more by attitude than by absolute circumstances. In their gratitude and satisfaction, the Morrels demonstrate humanity's capacity for goodness, which challenges Monte Cristo's condemnation of mankind as an "ungrateful" and generally vile species.

CHAPTERS 54–62

CHAPTER 54: ROBERT LE DIABLE

Monte Cristo and Haydée cause quite a stir when they appear in their box at the opera. Monte Cristo visits Madame Danglars's box, in which Eugénie, Albert, and Fernand are all sitting. While Monte Cristo leans over the balcony with Fernand, Haydée catches sight of the box and nearly faints. Monte Cristo takes leave of the

Danglars and Morcerf families and returns to Haydée, who is beside herself with emotion. She tells Monte Cristo that Morcerf is the man who betrayed her father, Ali Pacha, to the Turks and then sold her into slavery.

CHAPTER 55: A TALK ABOUT STOCKS
Albert de Morcerf and Lucien Debray visit Monte Cristo. They discuss Albert's engagement to Eugénie Danglars. Albert is reluctant to marry Eugénie, despite her extreme beauty and wealth, as she seems "too erudite and masculine." In addition, Mercédès is very upset at the prospect of having Eugénie as a daughter-in-law, and Albert cannot imagine doing anything to cause his mother pain.

Debray then reveals that Madame Danglars, his lover, gambles large sums of her husband's money in stocks. Albert jokingly suggests teaching Madame Danglars a lesson by manipulating her stocks with a false news report. Monte Cristo notices that Debray appears unsettled by this line of conversation. It is clear that Debray does, in fact, regularly abuse his government position by giving privileged information to Madame Danglars.

CHAPTER 56: MAJOR CAVALCANTI
Monte Cristo plans to meet with two men and instructs them to play the roles he has outlined for them in return for significant monetary compensation. The older man must pretend to be Marquis Bartolomeo Cavalcanti, a retired Italian major and nobleman who has been searching in vain for his kidnapped son for fifteen years.

CHAPTER 57: ANDREA CAVALCANTI
Monte Cristo continues that the younger man must play the part of Bartolomeo Cavalcanti's son, Andrea Cavalcanti, reunited with his father by Monte Cristo. After giving the two men false identity documents, new wardrobes, and other necessities for their disguise, Monte Cristo invites them to a dinner party he is throwing the following Saturday.

CHAPTER 58: AT THE GATE
Maximilian and Valentine meet again in the garden of the Villefort home. Maximilian reveals that Franz is returning to Paris soon, and Valentine swears that she is unable to oppose her father's will that she marry Franz. Valentine mentions that her stepmother wants her to remain unmarried and join a convent so that all of her inheritance will go to Edward, who will otherwise receive almost no inheritance at all. In the course of the conversation, it becomes clear that Eugénie

is just as reluctant to marry Albert de Morcerf as he is to marry her. Eugénie has confided in Valentine that she never wants to marry but wants instead to lead a free and independent life as an artist.

CHAPTER 59: M. NOIRTIER DE VILLEFORT

While Maximilian and Valentine hold their secret tryst, Villefort and his wife visit the room in their house in which Noirtier lives with his devoted servant, Barrois. Noirtier's stroke has left him with only the powers of sight and hearing, so he is unable to communicate with anyone but Villefort, Barrois, and Valentine. Valentine is Noirtier's sole happiness in life; because of her love and devotion, she is able to read all of her grandfather's thoughts and desires in his eyes. Villefort and his wife break the news of Valentine's engagement, and Noirtier is silently enraged, since Franz's father was his greatest political enemy. Valentine is sent to comfort her grandfather, and she confides in him that she does not want to marry Franz. Noirtier vows that he will help Valentine escape her unwanted engagement.

CHAPTER 60: THE WILL

Noirtier summons a notary and rewrites his will. He provides that if Valentine marries Franz, all of his inheritance will go to the poor rather than to Valentine. Villefort is unmoved by his father's threat and refuses to call off Valentine's engagement.

CHAPTER 61: THE TELEGRAPH

Downstairs, the Villeforts find Monte Cristo waiting for them. Monte Cristo invites them to his upcoming dinner party and tells them that he would like to visit a telegraph office. They suggest that he visit the Spanish line, which is the busiest.

CHAPTER 62: THE BRIBE

Monte Cristo visits a remote telegraph post, where he bribes the operator to pass along a false report. The next day, Debray hurries to the Danglars household and tells Madame Danglars that her husband must sell all of his Spanish bonds. Debray has just learned—in advance because of his government position—of a telegraph that came in announcing that a revolution is about to break out in Spain.

Madame Danglars follows Debray's advice. That evening's newspaper confirms the news about Spain, and Danglars saves a fortune as Spanish bonds plummet. However, the following day the newspaper states that the previous report of impending unrest was mistaken, stemming from an improperly intercepted telegraph communication. Danglars ends up losing one million francs.

ANALYSIS: CHAPTERS 54–62

The scene at the opera in Chapter 64 provides a sharp juxtaposition of two opposing elements of *The Count of Monte Cristo*. On one hand, the story is a fantastical melodrama, with a vampirelike count, a beautiful Greek princess, horrible betrayals, and breathtaking acts of revenge. On the other hand, it is a highly realistic novel, depicting the customs, hypocrisies, and everyday lives of French nobility. Dumas himself saw his novel as essentially a tale of contemporary manners, taking great care to provide the characters with real addresses, real restaurants, and stores to frequent, along with behavior authentic to their social status. Even the opera Monte Cristo attends is carefully chosen: *Robert Le Diable,* an 1831 work by Jacques Meyerbeer, is a performance that the upper crust of Dumas's time would certainly have turned out to see. Dumas even goes so far in his realism as to engage in some mild social satire. He mocks contemporary notions of propriety, for instance, by noting that while it would have been considered a scandal if Madame Danglars and her daughter had attended the opera alone, it is considered perfectly appropriate for them to be accompanied by Madame Danglars's lover, Debray. Dumas's impressive realism gives his novel a depth that a mere melodrama would not possess.

Dumas portrays Noirtier as one of the sympathetic characters of the novel, which is strange in light of Dumas's concern for individual liberties. In his days as a revolutionary, Noirtier committed the high sin of sacrificing individual lives to big ideas. In Villefort's words, he was a man "for whom France was a vast chessboard, from which pawns, rooks, knights, and queens, were to disappear, so that the king was checkmated." In other words, Noirtier treated people as means toward that which he considered an important end. Perhaps Dumas pardons Noirtier because he violated individual rights only with the eventual aim of securing such rights. As a revolutionary leader, Noirtier fought for the common people and for liberal, democratic ideals. In addition, because he is poised perfectly to do harm to Villefort, one of the novel's least sympathetic characters, Noirtier must, by default, have a redeeming character.

The telegraph episode of Chapters 61 and 62 is one of the only events in the long and drawn-out destruction of Danglars that Dumas actually portrays. Unlike the downfalls of Fernand and Villefort, which occur in brilliant bursts of spectacle, Danglars's downfall is slow and dull. Since Danglars cares about nothing but his wealth, it is his wealth that Monte Cristo attacks, causing repeated losses that destroy Danglars's credit. For the most part, Dumas gives us the behind-the-scenes story of Danglars's destruction in small hints. Various long-standing clients of Danglars suddenly borrow large amounts of money and then go bankrupt, unable to honor their debts to him. These long-standing clients, we are to understand, are all Monte Cristo borrowing under assumed names.

CHAPTERS 63–67

CHAPTER 63: SHADOWS

The guests arrive at the house in Auteuil for Monte Cristo's dinner party. The entire house has been decorated magnificently. Only two parts of the home have been left unchanged: the garden in the back and a small bedroom. Maximilian Morrel arrives first, followed by the Danglars, accompanied, as always, by Lucien Debray. Next, Monte Cristo introduces the two impostors as Major Bartolomeo Cavalcanti and his son, Andrea. Much as Monte Cristo predicts, the fabulously wealthy Italian prince and his son pique Danglars's curiosity, especially when Monte Cristo casually mentions to Danglars that Andrea is determined to find a wife in Paris. Finally, Villefort and his wife arrive.

Bertuccio, peeking out at the scene through a partly open door, is shocked when he sees Madame Danglars among the guests. He tells Monte Cristo that she is the widowed baroness who used to meet Villefort in this very house. Bertuccio is even more surprised to see Villefort himself, whom he thought he had killed years before. Monte Cristo explains that Villefort was only injured, not killed, when Bertuccio stabbed him. Bertuccio's greatest surprise, though, comes when he lays eyes on the man pretending to be Andrea Cavalcanti, as this man is actually his wayward son, Benedetto.

CHAPTER 64: THE DINNER

After dinner, Monte Cristo leads the party to the one bedroom he has left unchanged. He announces to his guests that he has felt, from the first moment he stepped inside, that some horrible crime was committed in this room. He begins to describe the scene he imagines took place here, which is, of course, the scene he knows actually did take place here. He imagines that a mother (Madame Danglars), who has just given birth, and a father (Villefort) take a child down the staircase. Monte Cristo then takes his guests, who include both Villefort and Madame Danglars, down into the garden and shows them the spot where, he claims, while working on his trees, he dug up the skeleton of a newborn baby. Deciding that he has pushed the murderous couple as far as he wants, Monte Cristo redirects the party back to the lawn for coffee. Villefort whispers to Madame Danglars that he must see her the next day in his office.

Chapter 65: The Beggar
After the party, as Benedetto climbs into his carriage, he is stopped by an old acquaintance from his former life, Caderousse. Caderousse, who has escaped from the prison where he was serving a life sentence for the murders he committed, demands that Benedetto give him an allowance of 200 francs each month. Benedetto, worried that Caderousse might jeopardize his newfound position, reluctantly agrees.

Chapter 66: A Conjugal Scene
Back home from the party, Madame Danglars retires to her room with Debray in tow. Unexpectedly, her husband bursts into the room and asks Debray to leave. Debray and Madame Danglars are shocked, since Danglars has never before opposed his wife's wishes. With Debray gone, Danglars confronts his wife. He knows that Debray supplies her with inside information, which she then leaks to him. He also knows that Debray pockets Madame Danglars's share of the investment earnings. Danglars does not mind this arrangement so long as Debray's information consistently wins him money, but now that he has lost a considerable sum on the Spanish bonds, he resents that Debray is not helping to defray the costs he incurred. Danglars also reveals that he knows about all of his wife's previous lovers, including the lovers she had during her first marriage. Most important, he knows that she bore Villefort's child and that her first husband killed himself as a result.

Chapter 67: Matrimonial Plans
The following day Danglars visits Monte Cristo and presses for more information about Andrea Cavalcanti. He admits that he would very much like his daughter to marry this young man, who is far richer than Albert de Morcerf. Danglars confides in Monte Cristo that the Count de Morcerf was not originally a nobleman but used to be a poor fisherman named Fernand Mondego, who suddenly gained considerable wealth under mysterious circumstances. Monte Cristo pretends to recall that he has once heard of a Fernand Mondego in connection with the Ali Pacha affair in Greece. Danglars

admits that he too has heard vague stirrings about this connection. Monte Cristo encourages Danglars to get in touch with his contacts in Yanina, the site of the Ali Pacha affair, and to make inquiries into the nature of Mondego's involvement.

ANALYSIS: CHAPTERS 63–67

The scene in Monte Cristo's bedroom and garden at Auteuil is born from the Romantic fascination with the Gothic and the grotesque. Monte Cristo paints a chilling scene for his audience, complete with a dark night, a secret staircase, an illicit love affair, and an act of infanticide. Gothic romances were extremely popular in the nineteenth century and had a strong influence on Dumas and other Romantic writers. Dumas plays up Madame Danglars's hysteria and Villefort's terror at hearing Monte Cristo's story to chilling effect, leaving us almost sympathetic for these two evildoers. Like the heroes and heroines of Gothic novels, Villefort and Madame Danglars are faced with a seemingly supernatural, terrifying, and inescapable force in the person of Monte Cristo. In this respect, though it is also a novel of contemporary manners and a fantastical melodrama, *The Count of Monte Cristo* is a good example of Gothic literature.

The scenes in this section also indicate that Monte Cristo's two most trusted companions, Bertuccio and Haydée, share his overwhelming desire for revenge. Bertuccio wants to avenge himself on Villefort because of his refusal, as public prosecutor, to seek justice in the murder of Bertuccio's brother. Haydée wants to take revenge on Fernand Mondego for betraying her father and selling her into slavery. It is, of course, convenient for Monte Cristo that his own enemies overlap with the enemies of his friends. Haydée and Bertuccio both have information and contacts that can help bring about the downfall of their mutual enemies, and they are willing to do whatever is required of them to accomplish this downfall. Yet it seems that Bertuccio and Haydée are not merely convenient to Monte Cristo but also enormously important to him as his only two true companions. However, it may be merely their common lust for revenge that draws Monte Cristo toward Bertuccio and Haydée. Monte Cristo is himself so obsessed with revenge that perhaps he cannot be truly comfortable around anyone who does not share this obsession to some degree.

Though Monte Cristo seems quite comfortable in the company of Bertuccio and Haydée, it is misleading to speak of him as having any close relationship—platonic or romantic—with another human being. Monte Cristo has willfully exiled himself from human society. He isolates himself to an extreme, living above the law, without a homeland, and without any emotional attachments. In Chapter 49, Monte Cristo describes himself to Villefort as "being of no country, asking no protection from any government, acknowledging no man as my brother." His refusal to acknowledge himself as a member of any country, society, or fraternity indicates that he has rejected membership in every conceivable community. None of these communities, Monte Cristo implies here and elsewhere, live up to his strict standards of justice and propriety. As a solitary being, unable to find a spiritual home anywhere in the modern world, Monte Cristo is a familiar type of Romantic hero. The theme of spiritual exile from the modern world was a popular one in the Romantic era, and famous nonconformists like Prometheus—the mythical Greek hero who stole fire from the gods to give to humans—and Satan frequently turn up as characters in Romantic prose and poetry. Monte Cristo, like other popular Romantic heroes, is the inveterate renegade, both rejecting and rejected by society.

CHAPTERS 68–76

CHAPTER 68: THE OFFICE OF THE PROCUREUR DU ROI
Madame Danglars visits Villefort's office, cursing their terrible luck at having their past dredged up again. Villefort, however, swears that the situation has nothing to do with luck. Monte Cristo, he explains, could not have found the skeleton of their child because the man who stabbed Villefort—Bertuccio—stole the box with the corpse from Villefort. He deduces that the child must have still been alive; if it had been dead, Bertuccio would have shown its corpse to the police and had Villefort arrested for murder as soon as he realized Villefort was still alive.

Concluding that the child must in fact still be alive, Villefort and Madame Danglars understand that they are in much danger. The fact that Monte Cristo seems to know of their crime makes their situation even more perilous. Villefort promises Madame Danglars that he will discover who the Count of Monte Cristo really is and find out how he knows so much about their past.

CHAPTER 69: A SUMMER BALL
That same day, Albert de Morcerf visits Monte Cristo and invites him to his family's ball.

CHAPTER 70: THE INQUIRY

Making inquiries through his police contacts, Villefort discovers that Monte Cristo has two old acquaintances living in Paris. The first is an Italian priest named Abbé Busoni, the other an English aristocrat named Lord Wilmore. Villefort sends the police commissioner to visit Busoni first. Busoni (Monte Cristo in disguise, of course) says that he has known Monte Cristo for decades and reveals that Monte Cristo is really the son of a rich Maltese shipbuilder. He mentions that Monte Cristo's only enemy is Lord Wilmore.

Villefort visits Wilmore himself. Wilmore (again, Monte Cristo in disguise) claims that Monte Cristo is a speculator who made his vast fortune when he discovered a silver mine in the Middle East. When asked why Monte Cristo has purchased the house in Auteuil, Wilmore explains that Monte Cristo hopes to dig up a mineral spring in the area. Villefort is relieved by this information.

CHAPTER 71: THE BALL

Monte Cristo is the center of attention at the Morcerfs' ball. Mercédès notices that he refuses to eat or drink anything the entire evening.

CHAPTER 72: BREAD AND SALT

Mercédès draws Monte Cristo away from the crowd and tries to coax him into eating some fruit from the garden. She becomes agitated when he refuses, perhaps because she knows that it is an Arabian custom that those who have eaten together beneath the same roof are eternal friends. Monte Cristo and Mercédès discuss their past in a roundabout way, never explicitly acknowledging that either is aware of the other's old identity. Monte Cristo promises that he considers Mercédès a friend. Villefort appears in search of his wife and daughter, bearing the terrible news that his former father-in-law, the Marquis de Saint Méran, is dead.

CHAPTER 73: MADAME DE SAINT-MÉRAN

That same night, the Marquise de Saint-Méran becomes sick, and the next morning she announces that she is going to die. She describes that during the night she saw a white figure approach her bed and heard it move the glass on her nightstand. The marquise yearns to see Valentine married before she dies and orders that the marriage contract be signed the day after Franz d'Epinay returns to France. Valentine longs to tell her grandmother that she loves another man but knows that her aristocratic grandmother would never allow her to marry a man from a family as common as Maximilian's.

CHAPTER 74: THE PROMISE

Valentine finds Maximilian waiting for her in the garden. He tells her that Franz has arrived in Paris and asks her to run away with him. After some coaxing, she agrees. That night, Maximilian waits for Valentine, armed with all they need for their escape, but she does not appear. Terrified that something has happened to her, he approaches the house and overhears a conversation between Villefort and a doctor. The marquise has died, and the doctor is convinced that she was poisoned with brucine.

The doctor suggests that the marquis and marquise might have accidentally been given a preparation intended for Noirtier, as Noirtier regularly takes brucine in small doses to alleviate his paralysis. Overcome with anxiety about Valentine's well-being, Maximilian sneaks into the house and finds her. Valentine introduces Maximilian to her grandfather. Noirtier tells Maximilian that he has a secret plan to prevent Valentine from marrying Franz.

CHAPTER 75: THE VILLEFORT FAMILY VAULT

Immediately following the burial of the marquis and marquise, Franz d'Epinay comes to the Villefort home to sign the marriage contract. Just as they are about to sign, Barrois appears and says that Noirtier wishes to speak to Franz.

CHAPTER 76: A SIGNED STATEMENT

Noirtier instructs Barrois to open a secret compartment in his desk and to hand Franz a stack of papers. The papers reveal that Noirtier killed Franz's father in a duel. Villefort flees in shock.

ANALYSIS: CHAPTERS 68–76

With his vast resources and hidden identities, Monte Cristo is a plausible forerunner of the modern superhero, using his enormous gifts to fight crime and help the innocent. Additionally, he is able to go incognito instantly and effortlessly, merely by donning a simple disguise. Dressed as an Italian priest or an Englishman, no one recognizes him as the Count of Monte Cristo. In Chapter 70, his red wig and fake scar so convince Villefort that he is Lord Wilmore that Villefort does not even begin to suspect his true identity. Perhaps the most impressive aspect of Monte Cristo's disguises is that they fool even his closest companions. Bertuccio, for instance, never figures out that Monte Cristo and Abbé Busoni are the same person. Monte Cristo's expert ability to disguise himself, along with his enormous strength and his seemingly inexhaustible knowledge, make him appear superhuman.

Monte Cristo can also be seen as a precursor to another popular modern figure, the detective. Monte Cristo meticulously assembles his enemies' histories, collecting clues and evidence by slyly questioning his suspects and those close to them, wheedling out of them any information they can give. He cleverly manipulates those around him, pressuring his enemies to their breaking point—tempting Danglars into betrothing his daughter to Cavalcanti, for instance, and subtly influencing Madame de Villefort to begin her campaign of murders. Eventually, Monte Cristo brings to light heinous crimes that, if not for his sleuthing, might never be uncovered.

Unlike his real-life model, Piçaud, Monte Cristo does not stoop to criminal actions when taking revenge. Instead, what we see unfolding in these chapters is an elaborate plan to destroy his enemies by exposing their own past crimes. Moreover, Monte Cristo does not rely on the crimes his enemies committed against him long ago, but instead draws on far greater crimes they have committed against others in the intervening years. Danglars is ultimately punished for his cruel financial opportunism, Fernand Mondego for his betrayal of Ali Pacha, and Villefort for his merciless and hypocritical wielding of the law. Seen in this light, it is not Monte Cristo who is the undoing of these men; it is rather their own criminal or selfish actions that are their own undoings. This distinction raises Monte Cristo's scheme from the level of petty revenge to the level of divine Providence. As we later see, he appeals to his enemies' particular weaknesses in tempting them into ruin. It is Danglars's greed, for instance, that draws him to Andrea Cavalcanti—an attraction that later becomes the final blow in his destruction. Villefort's undoing, by contrast, is brought on by his strong, unbending ambition, which prevents him from permitting a criminal investigation to take place in his house, thereby allowing the murderer to remain at large, poised to strike again. Destroying each villain with his own weaknesses and his own crimes, Monte Cristo truly sets himself up as the dispenser of justice rather than just a petty man getting back at old enemies.

The revelation of the connection between Noirtier and Franz d'Epinay's father casts Villefort in an even worse light than ever before. We know that Villefort is aware of this connection, as it is the very murder he and Noirtier discuss in Chapter 12, when Villefort warns his father that the police are after him. It is clear that Villefort wants the marriage to take place precisely because he thinks that it will guarantee that his father's crime will never come to light. Once Franz is a member of the family no one would think to suspect Noirtier, and even if someone were to suspect Noirtier, surely Franz would not want to pursue such a line of inquiry. As always, Villefort is acting solely for the sake of his own ambition, sacrificing his daughter's future and the feelings of an innocent stranger to his own goals.

CHAPTERS 77–84

CHAPTER 77: PROGRESS OF M. CAVALCANTI THE YOUNGER

Monte Cristo and the man acting as Andrea Cavalcanti visit the Danglars's home. Eugénie escapes to her room to play music with her constant companion and music teacher, Louise d'Armilly. Danglars insists that Andrea be allowed to join in the two women's music-making. Albert then arrives. Danglars is excessively rude to him.

CHAPTER 78: HAYDÉE

On the way back to Monte Cristo's house, Albert laughs over Danglars's obvious preference for Andrea as a son-in-law. Albert then asks to meet Haydée. Monte Cristo assents to the meeting with the condition that Albert not mention the name of his father. Haydée tells Albert the tragic story of Haydée's childhood. Her father, Ali Pacha, was the ruler of the Greek state of Yanina until a French soldier, who had become Ali Pacha's right-hand man, surrendered Ali's castle to the Turks and then betrayed him, allowing him to be brutally murdered by his enemies. This Frenchman then sold Haydée and her mother into slavery. Her mother died soon thereafter, and Haydée was eventually liberated when Monte Cristo purchased her freedom. Albert is bewildered by the story, not realizing that his father is the treacherous Frenchman who betrayed Ali.

CHAPTER 79: YANINA

Villefort receives an angry letter from Franz, calling off the engagement. Noirtier changes his will yet again, leaving all his fortune to Valentine on the condition that she is never separated from him. Meanwhile, Fernand pays a visit to Danglars in order to finalize the engagement between Albert and Eugénie. Much to his dismay, Danglars tells him that he has changed his mind about the engagement. Though Fernand presses him, Danglars refuses to divulge the cause for his change of mind.

The next morning a small article appears in Beauchamp's newspaper, reporting that a man named Fernand betrayed Ali Pacha to the Turks. Though there are many people who bear the name

Fernand, and no one thinks to associate this article with the Count de Morcerf, Albert is convinced that the article is a libelous slander against his father. Despite Monte Cristo's pleas for Albert to show restraint, Albert orders Beauchamp to retract the article or else fight a duel. Beauchamp, who did not even write the offending article, asks for three weeks to investigate the matter before he is forced to decide between these two options.

CHAPTER 80: THE LEMONADE
Barrois fetches Maximilian on behalf of Noirtier. As Albert, Noirtier, and Valentine discuss plans for the future, Barrois, overcome with thirst, takes a drink from his master's lemonade. Almost instantly, he falls sick and dies. The doctor discovers that there is brucine in the lemonade. Though Noirtier has drunk some of the lemonade, he is not affected because the small amount of brucine he takes every day for his paralysis has given him a tolerance for the substance.

CHAPTER 81: THE ACCUSATION
The doctor deduces that the poison was almost certainly meant for Noirtier. He then concludes that Valentine must be the murderer, as she is the sole heiress of all the intended victims thus far.

CHAPTER 82: THE ROOM OF THE RETIRED BAKER
Caderousse summons Benedetto to his home. No longer satisfied with his 200 francs per month, Caderousse presses Benedetto for more. Benedetto reveals his suspicion that Monte Cristo is really his father and that he will receive a large inheritance. Caderousse hatches a plan to break into Monte Cristo's Parisian home while he is away at Auteuil.

CHAPTER 83: THE BURGLARY
The next day Monte Cristo receives an anonymous letter warning him of the robbery. He orders his entire staff to abandon the Paris house, leaving only himself and Ali, both fully armed. After several hours, a man enters through the bedroom window. Ali notices another man keeping watch outside. Monte Cristo watches as the first man tries to break into his desk. He realizes, with surprise, that the thief is Caderousse. Monte Cristo quickly changes into his Abbé Busoni disguise and presents himself to Caderousse. Caderousse recognizes the priest instantly and is terrified.

Abbé Busoni tells Caderousse that he will let him go free if he reveals the entire truth about how he escaped from prison and explains what he is doing here now. Caderousse explains that an Englishman named Lord Wilmore sent a file to Benedetto, Caderousse's companion in chains, and that the two of them filed off their shackles and escaped. He also admits that he is now in league with Benedetto, living off of his friend's newfound salary. Busoni feigns shock at learning that Benedetto's alter ego, Andrea Cavalcanti—the fiancé of Eugénie Danglars—is nothing but a convict. He declares that he will make this fact known immediately.

To prevent the secret from leaking out, Caderousse lunges at Busoni with a dagger, but the dagger bounces off the chain-mail vest that Monte Cristo is wearing underneath his habit. Busoni forces Caderousse to write a note to Danglars, informing him that his future son-in-law is a convict. He then lets Caderousse leave through the window through which he entered, telling him that if he makes it home safely, then God has forgiven him. Monte Cristo knows, however, that Benedetto is outside waiting to kill Caderousse.

CHAPTER 84: THE HAND OF GOD
Just as Monte Cristo predicts, Benedetto stabs Caderousse. Monte Cristo brings the injured Caderousse into his house, and Caderousse signs a statement naming Benedetto as his murderer. As Caderousse dies, Monte Cristo berates him for his evil ways, urging him to repent and acknowledge God. Caderousse refuses until Monte Cristo reveals that he is really Edmond Dantès, at which point Caderousse acknowledges the existence of Providence and then dies. The police begin an all-out search for Benedetto.

ANALYSIS: CHAPTERS 77–84
The death of Caderousse marks Monte Cristo's first tangible success in exacting vengeance and delivering justice. The rest of his triumphs now come in quick succession; in fact, each individual's impending downfall is perfectly set up at this point in the novel. Danglars is losing his fortune quickly, as many of his previously reliable creditors continue to default on their debt. Danglars is also about to fall into the trap Monte Cristo has set in the form of Andrea Cavalcanti, the disgraceful suitor of his daughter, Eugénie. Fernand Mondego's history is now known by at least a few people in France, and it is only a matter of time before it becomes widespread public knowledge. Villefort's home is beset by murders, and his illegitimate son, whom he has tried to kill, is loose somewhere in Parisian society. Though no one but Monte Cristo knows it yet, three lives are about to be utterly destroyed.

While, as we see earlier in the novel, Julie and Emmanuel Herbaut are living proof that human beings can be truly satisfied with their lives, Caderousse embodies human dissatisfaction. Caderousse illustrates one of Dumas's major ideas in the novel: that happiness depends more on attitude than on absolute circumstances. As Caderousse is at death's door, Monte Cristo catalogues the man's long history of dissatisfaction. Feeling himself unfairly stricken with poverty, Caderousse contemplated crime, but then Busoni appeared with an unexpected fortune. Though this fortune seemed tremendous at first, Caderousse soon grew used to it and longed for more, so he resorted to murder in order to double his fortune. Fate then smiled on him again and saved him from prison. He could have lived a happy, comfortable life leeching off of Benedetto, but he again quickly became dissatisfied and longed for more, deciding once again to resort to theft and murder. Monte Cristo's message is that Caderousse can never be truly satisfied with what he has and will always want more. Additionally, because he is lazy and dishonest, he will always resort to dishonorable means in order to acquire what he wants. With his persistent dissatisfaction, Caderousse is the unfortunate foil to Julie and Emmanuel.

Comparing Monte Cristo's behavior toward the dying Caderousse to the behavior a real priest would exhibit, we see the difference between Monte Cristo's idea of his divinely ordained mission of justice and the traditional Christian concept of justice. As Abbé Busoni confronts the dying Caderousse with his shortcomings, Caderousse murmurs, "what a strange priest you are; you drive the dying to despair instead of consoling them." These words remind us that Christianity preaches forgiveness and condemns revenge. Just as Monte Cristo sets himself up as a force independent of and at odds with modern society, he also sets himself up as independent of and at odds with traditional Christianity. Despite this clear rift between the nature of Monte Cristo's mission and the content of Christian doctrine, however, Dumas nonetheless makes ample use of Christian imagery and symbolism in the novel. We recall that Dantès has been transformed in a symbolic baptism, for instance, and that Monte Cristo is said to hail from the Holy Land. The very name "Monte Cristo," meaning "mountain of Christ," suffuses the entire novel with religious overtones. This mixture of skepticism toward and fascination with religion on Dumas's part was quite common among Romantic writers.

CHAPTERS 85–88

CHAPTER 85: BEAUCHAMP
Beauchamp arrives at Albert's home with bad news. He has just returned from a voyage to Yanina, where he has found incontrovertible proof of the allegations against Morcerf. Beauchamp promises to suppress this information due to his friendship with Albert. Albert is devastated by the revelation regarding his father but grateful to Beauchamp, whom he now forgives.

CHAPTER 86: THE JOURNEY
Monte Cristo invites Albert to travel with him to his home in Normandy. They spend three pleasant days at the coast before an urgent letter from Beauchamp summons Albert back to Paris. The letter includes a newspaper clipping, from a paper other than Beauchamp's, that links Morcerf's name with the Ali Pacha affair. Now there can no longer be any doubt that Albert's father is in fact the man accused of betraying Ali.

CHAPTER 87: THE TRIAL
Albert arrives at Beauchamp's house demanding information. Beauchamp tells him all he knows: a man came from Yanina bearing a stack of condemning documents and gave them to a rival newspaper editor. Since the article was printed, something even more damning has taken place. At the daily meeting of the Chamber, the government body to which Morcerf belongs, it was decided that an extensive investigation should be opened into the matter. At Morcerf's request, the investigation was set to begin that evening.

Beauchamp tells Albert that during the hearing, Haydée appeared and testified that Morcerf betrayed her father, Ali Pacha. She claimed that Morcerf allowed her father to be killed by his enemies, stole his treasures, and then sold Haydée and her mother into slavery. Haydée presented a document recording the fact that Monte Cristo had purchased her from the dealer who purchased her from Fernand Mondego. The document mentioned Mondego by name. Haydée further supported her claim by asserting that her father's betrayer had a scar on his right hand, a scar that Morcerf possesses. The judges of the Chamber subsequently found Morcerf guilty of the crimes alleged.

CHAPTER 88: THE CHALLENGE

Albert swears to Beauchamp that he will kill the man responsible for his father's disgrace or die trying. Beauchamp tries to dissuade Albert, but fails. He agrees to help Albert track down his enemy and, to that end, confides that Danglars had been making inquiries about Morcerf in Yanina.

Albert rushes to Danglars's house and challenges both Danglars and Andrea Cavalcanti to a duel. Danglars tells Albert that it was Monte Cristo who suggested he write to Yanina. Albert then realizes that Monte Cristo must have known all along about his father's past, since he has known all along about Haydée's past. He deduces that Monte Cristo must be behind the plot to expose his father and decides that Monte Cristo is the one he must challenge to a duel.

ANALYSIS: CHAPTERS 85–88

Albert's reaction to the revelation of his father's shameful past consists entirely of undirected rage and an overwhelming desire for violence. He makes it clear that he wants to kill someone and that he does not particularly care whom he kills. Initially, Albert is even willing to kill his best friend, Beauchamp, for the simple reason that Beauchamp is associated with the newspaper in which the defaming article first appears. Afraid that Danglars will refuse to fight, Albert challenges Andrea Cavalcanti to a duel, even though he knows full well that Andrea has nothing to do with Morcerf's exposure. Finally, when confronted with the fact that Monte Cristo is his true enemy, Albert remarks, "I only fear one thing, namely to find a man who will not fight." Albert's reaction, though hotheaded and irrational, fits well with the rugged individualism heralded in the novel. Albert desires to act because he does not want to be a pawn of fate or of any other powerful, unfriendly forces. His overwhelming desire is not so much to kill but rather to avoid passivity: he will act simply for the sake of acting, even if there is no rational reason to do so. In this strong drive to assert himself against the forces of fate that are attempting to oppress him, Albert resembles Monte Cristo.

It is unclear, however, to what extent Monte Cristo truly holds Albert accountable for the sins of his father. Initially, Monte Cristo shows a markedly strong aversion to Albert, recoiling when he first shakes his hand in Italy and clearly hating him for being Fernand's son. Franz d'Epinay notices this aversion and warns Albert to keep his distance from the mysterious Monte Cristo. Yet, as the story progresses, we see Monte Cristo reluctantly growing fond of Albert and struggling with his positive feelings for him. When Albert reveals his strong devotion to Mercédès in Chapter 55, for instance, declaring that he could never hurt his mother by marrying Eugénie, Monte Cristo seems irritated by the presence of such a noble sentiment in Albert. Monte Cristo is forced to acknowledge that Albert is a good man and should not be viewed merely through the lens of his father's sins.

When Fernand's downfall seems imminent, Monte Cristo even begins to feel pangs of pity for Albert. With Danglars's revelation to Monte Cristo that he has succeeded in obtaining the information from Yanina, for instance, Monte Cristo finds it impossible to look at Albert, and he turns away "to conceal the expression of pity which passed over his features." The fact that Monte Cristo whisks Albert off to Normandy just when the story about his father is about to break can itself be interpreted as an act of pity, as Monte Cristo may be trying to spare Albert the pain of witnessing his father's humiliation firsthand. Then again, we might just as easily see the trip to Normandy as an attempt to deprive Fernand of his son's support just when he needs it most. In the next chapter, Monte Cristo's attitude toward the duel only casts his feelings for Albert into further doubt.

CHAPTERS 89–93

CHAPTER 89: THE INSULT

Albert and Beauchamp rush to Monte Cristo's house, but are told that he is not receiving any visitors. However, the servant at the door reveals that Monte Cristo will be attending the opera that evening. Albert sends word to Franz, Debray, and Maximilian to meet him at the opera. He then goes to see Mercédès and asks her whether she knows of any reason why Monte Cristo should consider Fernand his enemy. Mercédès tries to convince her son that Monte Cristo is not an enemy and begs him not to quarrel with a man he so recently considered his friend.

After Albert leaves Mercédès, she instructs a servant to follow him all night and report back to her about his activities. At the opera, Albert storms into Monte Cristo's box, insults him, and challenges him to a duel. The duel is set for eight o'clock the following morning and is to be carried out with pistols. Monte Cristo asks Maximilian and his brother-in-law, Emmanuel, to act as seconds, or assistants, at the duel.

CHAPTER 90: MERCÉDÈS

Mercédès pays a desperate visit to Monte Cristo. Monte Cristo explains to Mercédès why he hates Fernand, showing her the false accusation that Fernand personally mailed to the public prosecutor so many years before. Mercédès falls to her knees and begs his forgiveness, declaring her enduring love for Edmond Dantès. She pleads with Monte Cristo to save her son's life, beseeching him to take vengeance only on those who are guilty. Monte Cristo's vengeful will is broken, and he swears that Albert's life will be saved. However, his dignity requires that he still fight the duel, which means that he himself must die the next day.

CHAPTER 91: THE MEETING

Monte Cristo confides to Maximilian and Emmanuel that he plans to let himself be killed. He then demonstrates his almost superhuman skill with the pistol so that there will be no doubt as to whether he lost the duel on purpose. Albert finally arrives at the site of the duel, but rather than pick up his pistol he apologizes to Monte Cristo, telling him that he was right to avenge Fernand for wronging him. Monte Cristo realizes that Mercédès has told her son the entire story.

CHAPTER 92: THE MOTHER AND SON

Albert and Mercédès both plan to leave all their worldly possessions behind and create a new life away from the sins of Fernand. As they are about to depart their home forever, a letter from Monte Cristo arrives. Monte Cristo instructs Mercédès to travel to Marseilles, to the house in which Louis Dantès once lived. Buried under a tree in front of that house is the money that Dantès once planned to use to start a family with Mercédès. He writes that this money, though a pittance, is rightfully hers and should be enough to support her comfortably for the rest of her life. Mercédès accepts the gift and declares that she will use it as a dowry to gain entrance to a convent.

CHAPTER 93: THE SUICIDE

Monte Cristo comes home to Haydée, who has been eagerly awaiting him. He realizes that he might love Haydée as he once loved Mercédès. Just as they bask in each other's company, Fernand bursts in, enraged that his son did not follow through on the duel. Fernand then challenges Monte Cristo to a duel himself. Before fighting, Fernand demands to know who Monte Cristo really is. Monte Cristo disappears momentarily and then returns in the clothes of a sailor. Recognizing him instantly as Edmond Dantès, Fernand is stricken with terror and flees the house. He returns home to find his wife and son departing forever. As they pull away from the house, Fernand shoots himself in the head.

ANALYSIS: CHAPTERS 89–93

In these chapters, Mercédès demonstrates that she remains unchanged from the young woman she was in Marseilles, proving to Monte Cristo that he has been misjudging her all along. When Mercédès initially approaches Monte Cristo to beg for her son's life, she tries to win his sympathy by reminding him that she is still the same woman he once loved. With his response that "Mercédès is dead," Monte Cristo means to suggest that the innocent and good woman whom he once loved does not exist now as the wife of Fernand Mondego and perhaps never existed. Yet Mercédès proves wrong Monte Cristo's estimation of her, revealing her monumental strength of character when she tells Albert about his father's sins against Dantès. Her act requires incredible strength and courage, as it ensures that any last vestige of respect and love Albert bears his father will be destroyed. It would be understandable for Mercédès to allow Monte Cristo to die rather than harm her son's psyche any further, yet she unselfishly chooses to spare Monte Cristo's life.

Mercédès is often portrayed as the most intelligent character in the novel. Dumas notes that she is renowned all over Paris for her intelligence, and she is the only character able to unravel the mystery of Monte Cristo's identity immediately. When Mercédès saves Monte Cristo's life, she also proves herself the most noble character, the only one capable of forgiving those who may have done her wrong. She evokes even more sympathy by abandoning her wealth and comfortable life, refusing to live off of a fortune tainted by evil deeds. Convinced of Mercédès's enduring goodness and innocence, Monte Cristo forgives her completely and attempts to amend for the fact that he is effectively depriving her of her husband and her wealth. Monte Cristo is now fully convinced, just as we are, that Mercédès is as virtuous as ever.

The initial exchange between Monte Cristo and Mercédès highlights an important motif in the novel: the significance of names. Upon entering Monte Cristo's room, Mercédès addresses him as "Edmond," causing him to stumble in alarm. She then insists that he call her "Mercédès" and not "Madame de Morcerf," boldly defying Monte Cristo's assertion that Mercédès is dead. What they actually

SUMMARY & ANALYSIS

argue about here is whether or not they remain, on any level, the good and innocent people that they once were. In calling Monte Cristo "Edmond," Mercédès is proclaiming her belief that the kind and decent sailor she once knew still exists somewhere within the vengeful and mysterious Monte Cristo. By insisting that "Mercédès" is still alive, she is also trying to persuade Dantès that she remains the good woman whom he once loved—that despite his opinion, she has not become a greedy, haughty, and disloyal aristocrat.

The argument between Mercédès and Monte Cristo takes on an added layer of meaning when we consider the fact that their old names are the names of commoners while their new names are aristocratic titles. This detail links goodness with poverty and humility, as Dumas highlights a contrast between sincere, good, common folk and aristocrats who have become corrupted by wealth and power. Ultimately, both prove their enduring goodness: Monte Cristo by offering to die for Albert's sake, and Mercédès by saving Monte Cristo's life. They are both worthy of the identities that their old names connote. At their next meeting, they address each other by these names, reinforcing their essential goodness.

Chapters 94–102

Chapter 94: Valentine
After taking leave of Monte Cristo, Maximilian goes to see Valentine and Noirtier. He finds Valentine feeling ill and complaining that all drinks taste bitter to her. Their meeting is interrupted when Madame Danglars and Eugénie arrive, announcing that Eugénie will marry Andrea Cavalcanti in one week. Eugénie expresses her displeasure at being chained to a man rather than being allowed to live as an independent artist. Feeling progressively sicker, Valentine excuses herself and returns to Maximilian and Noirtier. While with them, she loses consciousness.

Chapter 95: The Confession
Maximilian runs to Monte Cristo and begs for help. Monte Cristo is indifferent to Valentine's plight at first, but when he hears that Maximilian loves her, he promises that he will save her life. Back in the Villefort home, the doctor communicates with Noirtier, who seems to understand what has happened. Noirtier confirms that Valentine, like all the others, has been poisoned. The only reason she is still alive is because he has slowly been accustoming her to successively larger doses of brucine, knowing that she would be the next victim.

As the doctor goes to examine Valentine, Monte Cristo rents the house next door to Villefort's in the guise of the Abbé Busoni.

Chapter 96: The Father and Daughter
Earlier that day, Eugénie confronts Danglars and declares that she will not marry Andrea Cavalcanti. Danglars confides in her that he is on the brink of financial ruin and that he needs the three million francs that his daughter's marriage with Cavalcanti will bring. Public knowledge that he will soon have this money at his disposal will be enough to restore his credit and allow him to borrow money in order to speculate in American railroads.

Eugénie agrees to go through with the signing of the marriage contract on the condition that her father merely use the report of the three million to restore his credit and not actually use any of Cavalcanti's money. Eugénie hints that there is a dramatic reason for her request, but Danglars loses all curiosity once he is assured that she will sign the marriage contract and thus ensure the return of his credit.

Chapter 97: The Contract
Three days later, a large party at the Danglars' residence celebrates the signing of the marriage contract. Just as the contract is being signed, Monte Cristo announces the existence of the letter written to Danglars by Caderousse. Monte Cristo claims that the letter has been found that very day in Caderousse's vest and that it has since been given to Villefort. He does not reveal the content of the letter, but as he finishes speaking, two gendarmes appear, looking to arrest Cavalcanti. Andrea (Benedetto in disguise), however, has disappeared.

Chapter 98: The Departure for Belgium
As the guests leave, Eugénie rushes to her room with Louise d'Armilly. The two women discuss their disdain for men and their plot to run away together to Italy by way of Belgium. Once in Italy, they plan to make a living from their music. They decide to leave that night. To prevent detection, Eugénie will dress as a man and pretend to be Louise's brother. Though Louise is frightened, Eugénie is fearless and doubtless. She cuts her hair and triumphantly dons masculine clothes. The two women pile their possessions into a carriage and ride away.

Chapter 99: The Hotel of the Bell and the Bottle
As Eugénie flees Paris, so does Benedetto. He stops overnight at an inn in the town of Compiègne, but oversleeps and wakes up to find

gendarmes milling around the hotel. Benedetto attempts to escape through the chimney of his room. Once on the roof, he must go down through another chimney, and he chooses the only one not emitting smoke. The room at the bottom of this chimney happens to be where Eugénie and Louise are staying. They give the alarm, and Benedetto is seized.

CHAPTER 100: THE LAW
Madame Danglars approaches Villefort, and she requests that he not pursue the case against Andrea Cavalcanti. For the sake of her family's dignity, Madame Danglars begs that Villefort simply make the affair go away. He rigidly refuses. At the end of their meeting, news comes that Cavalcanti has been arrested.

CHAPTER 101: THE APPARITION
Valentine has been sick for four days. On the fourth night, she sees a figure approach her bed. It is Monte Cristo, who explains that he has been keeping constant watch over her from his window next door. Whenever Monte Cristo sees poison put into her glass he enters her room, as he has done just now, and replaces the deadly contents with curative ones. Monte Cristo advises Valentine to pretend that she is asleep, then watch and wait in order to see who is trying to kill her.

CHAPTER 102: THE SERPENT
Valentine does as Monte Cristo says, and sees Madame de Villefort enter her room and pour poison into her glass. When Monte Cristo returns, Valentine expresses complete bafflement as to her step-mother's motive. Monte Cristo explains that Madame de Villefort wants Valentine's inheritance to go to Edward, Madame de Ville-fort's son. The saintly Valentine's first emotion is pity for Edward for having such ghastly crimes committed in his name. As Valentine is emotionally unable to denounce her stepmother, Monte Cristo hatches another plan to expose the murderess. He tells Valentine that no matter what happens she must trust him. He then gives her a tiny pill, which she swallows as he watches.

ANALYSIS: CHAPTERS 94–102
The news of Maximilian's love for Valentine has a profound effect on Monte Cristo, setting the scene for an emotional rebirth that is completed several chapters later. In response to Maximilian's admission, Monte Cristo "close[s] his eyes, as if dazzled by internal light."

This reference to an "internal light" suggests a sudden epiphany. Maximilian's love for Valentine opens up a possibility that Monte Cristo has never bothered to consider—that Valentine is innocent and does not deserve to die for her father's crimes. Until now, he has thought of Valentine as a placeholder, the child of Villefort, the "daughter of an accursed race." He is now forced to acknowledge that she is an independent, good person, bound up in her own life and in the lives of other good people. Though at this point Monte Cristo is still a firm believer in the justice of his cause, this episode is the first indication that he might not have quite enough knowledge to pull off his scheme perfectly. We see that he does not know everything about the people who will be affected by his actions.

Danglars and Benedetto, who are nearly joined as father and son-in-law, make a surprisingly well-suited unit. They share many of the same pathologies, caring about nothing except for money and willing to betray anyone who stands in their way of personal fortune. Danglars has no more qualms about selling Eugénie into a loveless marriage than he has earlier about sending Dantès to a life in prison. Benedetto, for his part, has been capable of torturing and killing the woman who raised him for the sake of a few gold coins. He has also showed readiness to kill the man he thinks is his father—Monte Cristo—in order to receive what he expects to be a vast inheritance.

Both Danglars and Benedetto are very adept at playing roles, pretending to be much better people than they truly are. We first saw Danglars's playacting in his interaction with Morrel, whom he manages to fool thoroughly enough to win a recommendation into the Spanish banking house where he wins his fortune. In Chapter 96, we learn that Danglars continues to play a part: "to the world and to his servants Danglars assumed the good-natured man and the weak father . . . in private . . . the brutal husband and domineering father." Likewise, Benedetto brings phoniness to a whole new level, becoming an actual impostor in his guise as Andrea Cavalcanti. Soon after, Benedetto behaves in a misleading manner similar to Danglars's, speaking "in the tone in which he had heard Dorante or Valère reply to Alceste in the Théâtre Français." The juxtaposition of their behaviors makes a clear point: these two greedy and deceptive men deserve to be each other's ruin.

In contrast to the conniving Danglars and Benedetto, Valentine is so guileless that she is incapable of grasping evil motives. When faced with the fact that her stepmother is trying to kill her, she cannot even begin to figure out why. Monte Cristo is forced to remind her that if she dies, all of her inheritance would go to Edward. Valentine's confusion signals her complete and trusting innocence and is reminiscent of Dantès's initial inability to understand how or why is imprisoned. However, whereas Dantès becomes vengeful when he discovers that he has enemies, Valentine does not. In fact, she so lacks a desire for revenge that she cannot even find it within herself to denounce the woman trying to murder her. Unlike Dantès's innocence, which passes quickly, Valentine's seems almost indestructible. Her innocence is not merely a function of youth and inexperience but an essential character trait that she simply cannot overcome. This trait, presumably, is one reason Valentine is consistently referred to as an "angel."

Eugénie poses a sharp and interesting contrast to Valentine's innocent passivity. Both Eugénie and Valentine long for the same thing—the freedom to choose how they live their own lives—yet each woman goes about achieving this goal in a very different way. Valentine balks at even the idea of opposing her father's will, and it takes an enormous amount of persuasion on Maximilian's part to persuade her to run away with him. That Valentine ultimately manages to marry the man she loves has nothing to do with her own actions, but depends entirely on the clever ruses devised by other people, namely Noirtier and Monte Cristo. Eugénie, by contrast, has no trouble standing up to her father, speaking boldly and calmly about her refusal to follow his orders. She displays no fear at all as she prepares to run away with Louise d'Armilly, enthusiastically embracing the prospect of finding her own way through Europe and making a career as an artist. Whereas Valentine lives an entirely passive life, depending upon other people to help her overcome any difficulties, Eugénie takes an active part in shaping her own destiny. Like Monte Cristo and Albert, she refuses to be a pawn of fate or any other external force, such as the expectations of her father or of society as a whole.

CHAPTERS 103–108

CHAPTER 103: VALENTINE

The next morning, Valentine appears to be dead. Madame de Villefort is the first one to enter Valentine's room. She throws the remaining liquid from the cup into the fire, then cleans out the cup. Yet when she returns later, once the rest of the household has been notified of Valentine's death, the glass is mysteriously filled again. The doctor immediately detects the poison in it. Madame de Villefort faints.

CHAPTER 104: MAXIMILIAN

Maximilian, unable to control himself in his grief, enters Valentine's room, disturbing Villefort as he kneels by his daughter's bed. Villefort, not knowing who Maximilian is, orders him to leave. Maximilian leaves, but then returns, carrying Noirtier in his wheelchair. Maximilian declares his love for Valentine, and Villefort extends his sympathy to him, bound by their common grief. Maximilian demands that Valentine's murder be avenged. Noirtier signals that he knows who the murderer is and asks to be left alone with his son. When the others are called back in, Villefort and Noirtier ask them to keep the crime secret for the time being. The priest from next door, Abbé Busoni, is then called in to pray over the body. Alone with Noirtier, Monte Cristo explains what is really taking place.

CHAPTER 105: DANGLARS'S SIGNATURE

Monte Cristo visits Danglars and sees that Danglars is making out five checks, each worth one million francs. Monte Cristo asks to have the checks. Though the money is intended for the hospital, Danglars reluctantly agrees, refusing to admit that he no longer has enough capital to make such large loans. As Monte Cristo leaves, the Commissioner of Hospitals arrives. He is astounded to learn that his five million francs have just been given to a single individual. Danglars promises that he will have the money for the hospital tomorrow. He has no real intention of paying, however, and plans to run away that very night in an attempt to escape his creditors.

CHAPTER 106: THE CEMETERY OF PÈRE-LA-CHAISE

At Valentine's funeral, Monte Cristo keeps careful watch over Maximilian. He follows Maximilian back to Julie and Emmanuel's house. There, Maximilian confesses that he is planning to kill himself. In an attempt to stop him, Monte Cristo reveals that he is really Edmond Dantès, the man who saved Monsieur Morrel from ruin. Overcome, Maximilian calls out to Julie and Emmanuel and tells them Monte Cristo's role in their lives. Monte Cristo stops Maximilian, however, before he can reveal Monte Cristo's true identity. Alone with Maximilian again, Monte Cristo plays upon his gratitude to extract a promise: for one month Maximilian will remain alive and never stray from Monte Cristo's side. If Maximilian is still unhappy at the end of this month, Monte Cristo will help him to commit suicide.

Chapter 107: The Division

The day after Danglars leaves, Madame Danglars rushes to Lucien Debray in a panic. She shows him the letter Danglars has left explaining his reason for running away. He has written that a series of strange events has left him bankrupt and unable to repay the debt to the hospital. Madame Danglars waits expectantly for some kind word from her lover, but he speaks to her merely as a business partner, handing over half the profits that they have made together using their illegal tricks to speculate with Danglars's fortune. It is clear that Debray wants no more to do with Madame Danglars now that she cannot provide him with access to Danglars's unlimited capital.

In another room in the same hotel where this scene is taking place, Albert and Mercédès plan out their future. Albert tells his mother that he has enlisted in the army. He gives her the check he has received upon joining and tells her to use part of it to travel to Marseilles, where the rest of her small savings is located. On their way out of the hotel they encounter Lucien Debray, who is struck by the contrast between Mercédès's and Madame Danglars's reactions to misfortune. Later the next day, Monte Cristo secretly watches as Albert puts his mother into a coach bound for Marseilles. He swears that he will restore these two innocent people to happiness.

Chapter 108: The Lions' Den

Bertuccio visits Benedetto in prison. Benedetto still expects to be saved by his powerful protector, the Count of Monte Cristo. He believes that Monte Cristo is his true father, a suggestion that disgusts Bertuccio. Bertuccio tells Benedetto that he is here to reveal the true identity of Benedetto's father, but they are interrupted before he is able to do so. He promises that he will return the following day.

Analysis: Chapters 103–108

Villefort's and Danglars's persistent vices lead them to suffer more severe punishments than they might otherwise face. Danglars's excessive greed motivates him to force his daughter into a marriage she does not want. He thereby loses both his daughter, as Eugénie justifiably flees a family that forces her to settle down against her will, and his dignity, suffering the public humiliation of nearly having an ex-convict for a son-in-law. Though Danglars would be financially ruined and utterly devastated even without these added blows, they certainly make his pain that much greater. Similarly, it is Villefort's excessive ambition that leads to the demise of his in-laws, his wife, his son, and—he thinks—his beloved daughter, Valentine. Villefort knows that a murderer is loose in his household, but he is also aware that, as a public prosecutor, widespread awareness of this murderer's existence could do his career and reputation great harm. Fearing the loss of dignity and the possible loss of his own power, he refuses to let an investigation take place until it is too late. In their reactions to Monte Cristo's schemes, we see that Danglars and Villefort are complicit in their respective downfalls, which underscores just how fully the men deserve their punishment. They have neither repented nor improved as they have aged.

Just as Eugénie and Valentine act as foils for each other, accentuating each other's characteristics, Madame Danglars and Mercédès also cut a striking contrast. There are obvious similarities between their situations, as both are now husbandless and publicly humiliated. Yet their attitudes could not be more different. Though Madame Danglars has actually played a large part in her husband's ruin, she feels as if she has been treated unfairly by fate. On the other hand, Mercédès, who has had no part in her husband's ruin, does not wallow in self-pity, although she *does* have a right to feel that fate has treated her unfairly. Rather than feel victimized, Mercédès feels that she has more wealth and luxury than she deserves. Despite her innocence, she ultimately abandons her vast fortune out of commitment to her personal honor. Lucien Debray notes this contrast between Madame Danglars and Mercédès, reflecting that "the same house had contained two women, one of whom, justly dishonored, had left it poor with 1,500,000 francs under her cloak, while the other, unjustly stricken, but sublime in her misfortune, was yet rich with a few deniers." Though Debray astutely notices the contrast, his focus is a bit off: what really differentiates the two women is not how rich they consider themselves, but how they react to their lowered status.

The contrast between Mercédès's graceful reaction and Madame Danglars's resentful reaction illustrates with an idea prominent in *The Count of Monte Cristo*: the importance of attitude in determining happiness or satisfaction. In objective terms, Madame Danglars is in a much better position than Mercédès: she is still enormously wealthy—as she has been siphoning money from her husband's fortune for years—and will be able to return to her old life in Parisian society in a matter of years. In addition, since Madame Danglars has no fondness for her husband, his loss is not particularly painful for her. Mercédès, on the other hand, is impoverished and will never be able to resume the comfortable life she once led. Additionally, though she is horrified by her husband's bad deeds, she has loved him and feels his loss acutely. Yet, while Madame Danglars endlessly bemoans her relatively benign circumstances, Mercédès does not lament her far worse fortune. She accepts the events of her life stoically and even considers them her just punishment for disloyalty to Dantès. In this respect, Madame Danglars is a parallel to Caderousse, making the worst of any situation, while Mercédès, like Emmanuel and Julie, exhibits the ability to overcome adversity with courage and acceptance.

CHAPTERS 109–113

CHAPTER 109: THE JUDGE

Villefort buries himself in work, building the case against Benedetto. On the day of the trial, he finally approaches Madame Villefort and makes clear that he knows she is a murderer. He tells his wife that he will not let her die on the scaffold, as that would bring shame to both himself and to his son. Villefort instead instructs her to take her own life, using the poison she used to commit her murders. If she has not done this by the time he returns from court, he warns, he will publicly denounce her and have the authorities execute her.

CHAPTER 110: THE ASSIZES

Benedetto's trial is a major event, and all of the fashionable Parisians turn out at the courthouse to watch. During the trial, Benedetto announces that he is the son of Villefort. He tells the story of his birth—how his father buried him alive, how a man then stabbed Villefort and stole the box in which he was buried, and how he was taken in and raised by adoptive parents. The court asks for proof, but Villefort interrupts and declares himself guilty.

CHAPTER 111: EXPIATION

> [H]e felt he had passed beyond the bounds of vengeance, and that he could no longer say, "God is for and with me."
>
> (See QUOTATIONS, p. 92)

On his way back home, Villefort regrets condemning his wife to death, realizing that he is no more innocent than she. He decides that he will let her live, and that they will flee France together. However, when he comes home, he finds that she has already followed his orders. In addition to killing herself, Madame Villefort has also killed Edward, unwilling to let her son live on without her.

Seeking solace, Villefort runs to see his father, Noirtier, who is accompanied by the Abbé Busoni. The Abbé reveals his true identity as Edmond Dantès. Grabbing him by the wrist, Villefort leads Dantès to the corpses of his wife and son, and he asks if Dantès's vengeance is complete now. At the sight of the dead boy, Dantès's face takes on a look of anguish. He tries to revive Edward with the powerful elixir that he uses earlier, but is unsuccessful. Dantès approaches Villefort in order to offer him comfort in the knowledge that Valentine is not really dead, but Villefort has apparently gone insane. For the first time, Dantès doubts the justice of the project he has been carrying out. Back at home, he tells Maximilian that they will leave Paris the next day.

CHAPTER 112: THE DEPARTURE
The next day Maximilian goes to say goodbye to Julie and Emmanuel. Monte Cristo comes to pick up Maximilian, and they leave Paris together. As they go, Monte Cristo looks out over the city and declares his work of vengeance done.

CHAPTER 113: THE HOUSE IN THE ALLÉES DE MEILLAN
Maximilian and Monte Cristo arrive in Marseilles in time to watch Albert board a ship bound for his military post in Africa. Maximilian goes to visit his father's grave, while Monte Cristo pays a visit to Mercédès, who is now living in the small house that Louis Dantès once inhabited. Maximilian promises Mercédès that he will help her son in any way he can. Mercédès expresses passive resignation toward her ill fate, claiming that it must be God's will. Monte Cristo chides her, reminding her that God created man with free will. Monte Cristo then meets Maximilian in the cemetery and tells him to wait in Marseilles in several days, since he must take care of some business in Italy.

ANALYSIS: CHAPTERS 109–113
Chapter 111 marks the second major turning point of *The Count of Monte Cristo,* the moment when Monte Cristo finally begins to doubt whether he is justified in taking the place of Providence. With Edward's death, the seeds of discomfort that are sown in Chapter 95—when Monte Cristo realizes that he could easily have caused

the death of the innocent Valentine—now bloom into full-fledged torment. Understanding that he has indirectly caused the end of an innocent life, Monte Cristo no longer feels that his actions are in total alignment with God's will. Having buoyed himself all along with the belief that his mission is ordained by God, this blow to his confidence is enormous. Some versions of the novel include a scene in which Monte Cristo returns to the Château d'If, looking for a sign that his mission of vengeance was justified. He finds this sign in the form of the Abbé Faria's manuscript, which begins with the biblical quote "Thou shalt tear out the teeth of the dragon and trample the lion's underfoot, thus saith the Lord." With this scene omitted, the justification for Monte Cristo's mission is never confirmed, leaving Monte Cristo hovering in doubt as to the morality of his mission.

The last act Monte Cristo makes before plunging headlong into doubt is his attempt to revive Edward using his elixir. This potion, with its seemingly magical ability to heal, is a symbol for Monte Cristo's hubris—his prideful belief that he, like his elixir, is capable of any feat. His hubris reaches its height in this scene, culminating in the assertion that his elixir actually gives him the power to bring a boy back to life. Of course, Monte Cristo is incapable of granting life, and his seemingly unassailable confidence in himself and his elixir is finally shaken.

Monte Cristo's final conversation with Mercédès pits his active approach to life against her passive resignation, and the former clearly emerges victorious. When Mercédès declares that she has "become passive in the hands of the Almighty," Monte Cristo counters that God does not approve of such resignation. Free will, Monte Cristo contends, is the thing that makes one human. Only by exercising one's will, asserting one's individual desires against the opposing forces of the world, can one please God. This conversation is tinged with a slightly accusatory undertone, since it is Mercédès's passive resignation that led her to marry Fernand Mondego against her own better judgment and her own desires. Lacking the courage to resist, she resigned herself to the fate she saw spread out before her rather than struggle for what she really wanted and knew was right. In her passivity, Mercédès stands in stark contrast to Monte Cristo, Eugénie Danglars, and her own son, Albert, all of whom try to take an individual stand against fate rather than passively resign themselves to what the world offers them.

It is worth noting that the two most passive characters in the novel, Mercédès and Valentine, are portrayed as models of femininity, while the proactive characters are primarily men. The only proactive female character is the excessively masculine Eugénie, who can be interpreted as a cross-dressing lesbian. Dumas suggests that passiveness is a female trait, noting that Valentine "could not understand that vigorous nature [of Eugénie's] which appeared to have none of the timidities of woman." Given that Dumas portrays an active stand against destiny as far superior to passive resignation—and his further implication that passive resignation, the cause of Mercédès's downfall, is even sinful—we can argue that Dumas is not overly generous to his female characters.

Suicide, a common motif of the novel as well as of Romantic literature in general, is presented as an obvious response to abandonment by a beloved. Even before Valentine falls ill, Maximilian has prepared to take his own life in the event that she ever marries Franz d'Epinay. As we see in the last chapter of the novel, Haydée proves her sincere affection for Monte Cristo by declaring that she will take her life if he leaves her. Yet the act of suicide—the most dramatic means of giving up the fight against fate—seems to fly in the face of Monte Cristo's stance against passive resignation. Maximilian provides a possible insight into this seeming inconsistency, as he explains that he wants to take his own life because "all [his] hopes are blighted." Monte Cristo considers hope the only thing that makes life worth living; thus, it is plausible that his ultimate judgment on suicide would be that once all hope is gone—as some people think it is when they lose their beloved—suicide may be reasonable, as there is nothing left for which to fight.

CHAPTERS 114–117

CHAPTER 114: PEPPINO

Danglars travels to Italy and presents Monte Cristo's receipt for five million francs to the firm of Thomas and French. He plans to use this money to resettle in Vienna rather than reimburse any of his creditors. Peppino, now one of Luigi Vampa's bandits, has been tipped off about the huge sum that Danglars is about to withdraw and follows Danglars to Thomson and French.

The next day, Vampa's bandits ambush Danglars as he rides from Rome to Venice. Danglars is presented to Vampa, who is busy reading Plutarch. Vampa places Danglars in a cell, comfortably made up with a bed. Danglars decides that the bandits would have killed him already if that had been their intent, so he concludes that he will most likely be held for ransom. As Danglars cannot imagine that the bandits would hold him for a sum anywhere near five million francs, he feels sure that all will work out well and goes to sleep contented.

CHAPTER 115: LUIGI VAMPA'S BILL OF FARE
The next day, Danglars is left alone in his cell and becomes extremely hungry. In response to his request for food, he is told that he can order any meal he wants, but that he must pay a ridiculously high price for it—one hundred thousand francs for any item. Reluctant but half-starved, he buys a chicken.

CHAPTER 116: THE PARDON
The next day Danglars asks to see Vampa. Vampa tells Danglars that he is keeping him captive under someone else's orders and, therefore, can do nothing to alter the food situation. After twelve days, Danglars has used up all but fifty thousand of his francs buying food and drinks. He decides that he will save this last bit of money at any cost, and for days he eats nothing.

Finally, Danglars cries out for mercy, feeling he can take the hunger no more. A strangely familiar voice asks him if he repents his evil ways, and he swears that he does. Monte Cristo steps into the light and tells Danglars that he is forgiven. He reveals his true identity and then tells Danglars that he is free to go. Dumped by the side of the road, Danglars draws himself to a brook in order to drink and notices that his hair has gone white from terror.

CHAPTER 117: THE FIFTH OF OCTOBER

> There is neither happiness nor misery in the world;
> there is only the comparison of one state with another.
> *(See* QUOTATIONS, *p. 93)*

On the day that Maximilian's one month expires, he meets Monte Cristo on the island of Monte Cristo and proves himself still eager to die. Monte Cristo leads Maximilian into the exquisite palace carved into the rocks, which is filled with every earthly delight. Monte Cristo tests Maximilian's resolve, attempting to determine whether his unhappiness is absolute and his devotion to Valentine limitless. Monte Cristo even offers Maximilian his entire fortune if he chooses life instead of death. Maximilian refuses the offer, wanting only release from the pain of lost love. Pretending to relent to Maximilian's wishes, Monte Cristo hands the young man a green liquid, which Maximilian assumes is poison. Maximilian drinks it down and falls into a deep sleep.

Valentine then comes running out. Monte Cristo tells her that she must never leave Maximilian's side, since he has been willing to die in order to be reunited with her. In return for bringing the two of them together, Monte Cristo asks Valentine to look after Haydée, as she will now be alone in the world. Haydée then appears and asks what Monte Cristo means. He explains that he is going to restore her to her position as a princess, and orders her to forget him and be happy. Haydée says that she would die if she had to leave him. Monte Cristo embraces her ecstatically, finally allowing himself to believe that he can be happy in love. He says he had intended to do penance by denying himself Haydée's company, but claims that this gift must be a sign that God has forgiven him. Monte Cristo and Haydée withdraw. Maximilian wakes up and finds Valentine waiting for him.

The next morning, Maximilian finds a letter left by Monte Cristo, who has already departed with Haydée. The letter instructs Maximilian and Valentine to sail to Leghorn, where Noirtier is waiting to lead Valentine to the altar. Monte Cristo has given the young couple all of his property in France, as well as his holdings on Monte Cristo, as a wedding present. Finally, the letter explains why Monte Cristo treated Maximilian as he did. There is no such thing as happiness or unhappiness in the world, he explains, but only the comparison of one state with another. Therefore, in order to know how good life truly is, one must, like Maximilian, have once wished for death. Monte Cristo's final words are that all human wisdom is contained in two words: wait and hope.

> [A]ll human wisdom is contained in these two
> words, — "Wait and hope."
>
> *(See* QUOTATIONS, *p. 94)*

ANALYSIS: CHAPTERS 114–117

Monte Cristo's timely pardon of Danglars, just before he starves to death, can be seen as an indication that Monte Cristo has finally recognized his limits as an agent of Providence. Realizing that he is not a substitute for God on earth, Monte Cristo appears to have decided that it is not his right to take away another man's life or sanity, neither of which can ever be regained. Though Danglars is left impoverished, he still has his life and his sanity, unlike Fernand and Villefort. This punishment is the least severe of the three, as it is possible to enjoy life without wealth and also possible to gain one's wealth back. In addition, by allowing Danglars to remain alive and sane, Monte Cristo is giving his enemy the chance to repent and be forgiven by God, an opportunity he does not give Villefort or Fernand. However, it could be argued that Monte Cristo has been planning to spare Danglars's life all along: although Danglars's punishment is less severe than those of Fernand and Villefort, it nonetheless perfectly fits his sins of greed.

Regardless of whether each punishment is precisely what Monte Cristo has intended, each is a perfect match for the nature of the crime it is intended to punish. Danglars betrays Dantès out of pure greed, motivated by his desire for the lucrative position as captain of the *Pharaon*. In the years succeeding Dantès's imprisonment, Danglars continues to live a life guided by such avarice. Money is the sole object of his desire and the cause of all his misdeeds, and so it is money of which he is ultimately deprived. Villefort, on the other hand, sentences Dantès to a life in prison because of his raw ambition and his mercilessness, so Monte Cristo leaves him without the coldly rational mind that earlier allows him to impose the law so brutally. Fernand, conversely, wants to ruin Dantès in order to win Mercédès for himself, and he is punished with the loss of the love and respect of his family, without which Fernand sees no reason to live and thus kills himself. Whether intended or coincidental, the perfect fit between crime and punishment in each case emphasizes how close Dantès comes to approximating Providence.

Dantès has barely seemed human ever since his discovery of the treasure on Monte Cristo and his embarkation on his voyage of revenge. He has taken no joy in life, and his emotions have been limited to gratitude and vengeful hatred. With Haydée's unexpected avowal of her love, however, Monte Cristo suddenly sees his chance to reenter the human world. Overcome with emotion, he tells Haydée, "through you I again connect myself with life, through you I shall suffer, through you rejoice." We see clearly that Monte Cristo's ability to reconnect with life requires that he feel love once again. With his father and Abbé Faria dead and Mercédès married to another man, Monte Cristo has lived without love for years. He has felt affection for Morrel, Maximilian, and Julie, but these feelings are more fondness and respect than any deep, meaningful connection. Without love, and thus without an intimate connection to any human being, Monte Cristo has been disconnected from humanity.

Now, with his love for Haydée requited, he can regain his full humanity and learn to "suffer" and "rejoice" again.

We may interpret Monte Cristo's final words about waiting and hoping as his final renunciation of his revenge project, an acknowledgment that only God can act with the authority of Providence, leaving human beings to wait and hope that God ultimately punishes the evil and rewards the good. These words, however, do not indicate that Monte Cristo is abandoning his strong belief in the right to try to shape one's own destiny, but merely that he is giving up the belief that one has the right to step in for God and irrevocably shape the destiny of others.

IMPORTANT QUOTATIONS EXPLAINED

1. "I regret now," said he, "having helped you in your late inquiries, or having given you the information I did."

   "Why so?" inquired Dantès.

   "Because it has instilled a new passion in your heart—that of vengeance."

This prophetic exchange occurs between Abbé Faria and Dantès in Chapter 17, immediately after Faria deduces the events surrounding Dantès's imprisonment. Until this moment, Dantès has been entirely ignorant of the evil done to him, believing that his misfortune is merely the result of incredibly bad luck. Once Faria reveals that Dantès has in fact been betrayed, Dantès's innocence is destroyed forever. He is confronted with the simple fact that evil exists, a fact he has never before considered. From this moment onward, Dantès begins a transformation from a kind and loving man into a vengeful and hate-filled one. This transformation has not yet begun, of course, at the time Faria expresses his regret. Yet Faria, with his thorough understanding of human nature, accurately predicts that Dantès will soon be consumed with the thought of the wrong done to him and will thirst for vengeance. He knows that once this transformation occurs, Dantès will never be able to experience life the way he does before he feels these emotions of bitter vengeance.

2. "I . . . have been taken by Satan into the highest mountain
    in the earth, and when there he . . . said he to me, 'Child of
    earth, what wouldst thou have to make thee adore me?' . . .
    I replied, 'Listen . . . I wish to be Providence myself, for I
    feel that the most beautiful, noblest, most sublime thing in
    the world, is to recompense and punish.'"

Monte Cristo makes this surprisingly frank admission to Villefort in
Chapter 49, during their initial reunion. Monte Cristo's obsession
with reward and punishment, which he here confesses, is the driving
force of the last two-thirds of the novel, and this statement provides
excellent insight into Monte Cristo's own concept of his mission.
What is particularly striking about this passage is its demonstration
that Monte Cristo associates his mission of vengeance not only with
God but also with the devil. His characterization of his mission as
both godlike and satanic is likely an attempt to frighten and unnerve
Villefort. Yet this characterization foreshadows Monte Cristo's later
realization that there is in fact something slightly evil to his mission
as well as something holy. Ultimately, Monte Cristo acknowledges
that only God has the right to act in the name of Providence, and
that, like the devil, he himself has overstepped his bounds by trying
to act in God's domain.

QUOTATIONS

3. [H]e felt he had passed beyond the bounds of vengeance,
    and that he could no longer say, "God is for and with me."

This statement appears in Chapter 111, when Monte Cristo discovers that Edward de Villefort has been killed. Edward is the first
innocent person whom Monte Cristo unwittingly strikes down, and
this tragic injustice casts Monte Cristo's entire project into doubt.
Though he has already come close to killing the angelic Valentine
and has destroyed the lives of the noble Mercédès and Albert, up to
this point, Monte Cristo has not wreaked any irreversible harm on
anyone unworthy of punishment. In a burst of clarity, Monte Cristo
realizes that, as a mere mortal, he is not capable of doling out retribution in such a way as to ensure that no innocents are harmed. He
is not omniscient or omnipotent and therefore cannot determine or
control what unforeseen effects his actions might have. For the rest
of the novel, Monte Cristo grapples with doubt, ultimately deciding that only God has the right to act in the name of Providence. In
order to atone for "pass[ing] beyond the bounds of vengeance,"
Monte Cristo attempts to help Valentine and Maximilian attain ultimate happiness.

QUOTATIONS

4.   "There is neither happiness nor misery in the world; there
     is only the comparison of one state with another, nothing
     more. He who has felt the deepest grief is best able to
     experience supreme happiness."

This passage appears in the parting letter that Monte Cristo leaves
for Maximilian in Chapter 117. Monte Cristo offers this analysis of
happiness as an explanation for his allowing Maximilian to spend
an entire month under the false impression that his beloved, Valentine, is dead. Monte Cristo believes that in order to experience
ultimate happiness, Maximilian first has to experience absolute despair, just as Monte Cristo himself has. Monte Cristo suggests that
only now that Maximilian has demonstrated a willingness to die in
order to be reunited with Valentine can he truly appreciate living
alongside her. It is clear that this swing from ultimate despair to
ultimate bliss not only pertains to Maximilian but also to Monte
Cristo, who has finally found ultimate happiness in Haydée's love,
decades after the ultimate despair of his days in prison. The notion Monte Cristo expresses here—that of the necessary connection
between ultimate misery and ultimate joy—recalls one of the main
ideas in *The Count of Monte Cristo*, the assertion that happiness
and unhappiness depend more on one's internal state of mind than
on one's external circumstances.

QUOTATIONS

5.   "[U]ntil the day when God will deign to reveal the future
      to man, all human wisdom is contained in these two
      words,—'Wait and hope.'"

This remark also appears in the final letter Monte Cristo leaves for
Maximilian in Chapter 117. These words represent Monte Cristo's
final renunciation of his project of vengeance. Until now, he has
considered himself God's agent on earth, attempting to carry out the
retribution that he believes God has appointed him to oversee. He
has effectively placed himself on a par with God, unwilling to allow
his mortal limits to prevent him from doling out divine justice. Yet
doubt over Monte Cristo's capacity and right to act as God's agent
has been building steadily ever since Edward's unjust death and has
finally resulted in a complete disavowal of the mission Monte Cristo
has just completed. Here, Monte Cristo acknowledges that God is
the only one who can act as Providence, the only force that can
hand out people's fates. Humans, rather than taking God's task into
their own hands, ought to simply "[w]ait and hope" that God does
indeed eventually reward the good and punish the bad.

KEY FACTS

FULL TITLE
: *The Count of Monte Cristo* (*Le Comte de Monte-Cristo,* in the original French)

AUTHOR
: Alexandre Dumas

TYPE OF WORK
: Novel

GENRE
: Adventure; Romantic novel; moralistic tale

LANGUAGE
: French

TIME AND PLACE WRITTEN
: 1844, France

DATE OF FIRST PUBLICATION
: Published serially from August 1844 until January 1846

PUBLISHER
: *Le Journal des Débats*

NARRATOR
: The novel is narrated by an anonymous voice.

POINT OF VIEW
: The narrator speaks in the third person, focusing almost entirely on outward action and behavior rather than delving into the psychological realities of the characters.

TONE
: The narrator is detached from the story, relating the events as they happen.

TENSE
: Present

SETTING (TIME)
: The novel takes place during the years following the fall of Napoleon's empire. The story begins in 1815 and ends in 1844.

SETTING (PLACE)

Though most of the action takes place in Paris, key scenes are also set in Marseilles, Rome, Monte Cristo, Greece, and Constantinople.

PROTAGONIST

Edmond Dantès

MAJOR CONFLICT

Unjustly imprisoned, Dantès's seeks to punish those responsible for his incarceration; as the vengeful Count of Monte Cristo, he struggles to transcend his human nature and act as an agent of divine retribution.

RISING ACTION

In prison, Dantès meets Abbé Faria, who unravels the mystery of Dantès's downfall; Dantès vows to spend his fortune on an obsessive quest to reward those who have been kind to him and to punish those who have harmed him; Dantès visits Caderousse and confirms the details of the events leading up to his incarceration; Dantès eases himself into the lives of those responsible for his time in prison.

CLIMAX

Dantès slowly brings complete devastation upon Caderousse, Fernand, Villefort, and Danglars.

FALLING ACTION

Dantès enables the blissful union of Maximilian Morrel and Valentine Villefort; Dantès finally opens himself to emotions other than gratitude and vengeance and admits his love for Haydée.

THEMES

The limits of human justice; relative versus absolute happiness; love versus alienation

MOTIFS

Names; suicide; politics

SYMBOLS

The sea; the red silk purse; the elixir

FORESHADOWING

Abbé Faria's apology to Dantès; the painting of Mercédès looking out to sea suggests her undying love for Dantès.

Study Questions

1. *Dumas often writes of Edmond Dantès's time in prison as if it were a death. What do you think is the significance of this choice of language?*

Though Dantès does not physically die in prison, he does lose nearly all of his previous character traits. He enters prison innocent, honest, kind, and loving, but leaves it bitter, vengeful, and full of hate. What really seems to die within Dantès is his basic humanity. He is left without compassion and without the capacity to experience normal human emotions, such as sadness, joy, and remorse. It is not Dantès's experience of prison itself that causes this transformation but rather his knowledge that he is suffering this miserable fate because of evil done to him by other human beings. Dantès's desire for vengeance acts as a poison, killing the pleasant side of him and leaving only spite.

2. *Describe how* The Count of Monte Cristo *reflects the nineteenth-century Romantics' obsession with the exotic.*

Dumas was well known as a travel writer long before he began writing fiction, and we can see this talent for painting exciting portraits of exotic locales in *The Count of Monte Cristo*. The novel begins in Marseilles, a provincial town in the south of France, a place in itself somewhat exotic to most of Dumas's readers. The story then moves to Italy, a favorite exotic spot for French writers to depict. Dumas's portrait of Italy expertly combines the shocking and foreign—the bandits, the execution, and the carnival—with expected stereotypes such as the hotel owner. Though the bulk of the rest of the novel takes place in Paris, there are fantastical interludes set in both Greece and Constantinople.

It is not only the novel's locales but also the people represented that make *The Count of Monte Cristo* so satisfyingly exotic. Haydée, with all her foreign beauty and mystery, is a model of the Oriental ideal the Romantics upheld. Likewise, Monte Cristo's own associations with the East augment his mystique. On several occasions he professes to consider himself more Eastern than Western, and many of his intriguing customs, such as his refusal to eat or drink in the home of an enemy, are Eastern in origin. Even Fernand and Mercédès can be considered exotic because, as Catalans, they are actually of Spanish rather French descent.

3.   *Monte Cristo's last words to Maximilian are "Wait and hope." What is the significance of this statement? How does it connect to the larger narrative of the novel?*

From the time that Edward de Villefort dies, Monte Cristo grapples with doubt about the justice of his mission. The death of an innocent boy is clearly not a just outcome; it casts a shadow on Monte Cristo's entire project. Monte Cristo's parting statement to Maximilian, then, can be seen as a final renunciation of his project, an acknowledgment that God is the only one who can act as Providence and decide people's fates. Rather than try to carry out justice themselves, human beings should simply "[w]ait and hope" that God really does ultimately reward the evil and punish the good. Monte Cristo is not abandoning his strong belief in a person's right to try to shape his or her own destiny, but he is giving up the belief that a person has a right to step in for God and shape the destiny of others.

How to Write
Literary Analysis

The Literary Essay: A Step-by-Step Guide

When you read for pleasure, your only goal is enjoyment. You might find yourself reading to get caught up in an exciting story, to learn about an interesting time or place, or just to pass time. Maybe you're looking for inspiration, guidance, or a reflection of your own life. There are as many different, valid ways of reading a book as there are books in the world.

When you read a work of literature in an English class, however, you're being asked to read in a special way: you're being asked to perform *literary analysis*. To analyze something means to break it down into smaller parts and then examine how those parts work, both individually and together. Literary analysis involves examining all the parts of a novel, play, short story, or poem—elements such as character, setting, tone, and imagery—and thinking about how the author uses those elements to create certain effects.

A literary essay isn't a book review: you're not being asked whether or not you liked a book or whether you'd recommend it to another reader. A literary essay also isn't like the kind of book report you wrote when you were younger, where your teacher wanted you to summarize the book's action. A high school- or college-level literary essay asks, "How does this piece of literature actually work?" "How does it do what it does?" and, "Why might the author have made the choices he or she did?"

The Seven Steps

No one is born knowing how to analyze literature; it's a skill you learn and a process you can master. As you gain more practice with this kind of thinking and writing, you'll be able to craft a method that works best for you. But until then, here are seven basic steps to writing a well-constructed literary essay:

1. Ask questions
2. Collect evidence
3. Construct a thesis

4. Develop and organize arguments
5. Write the introduction
6. Write the body paragraphs
7. Write the conclusion

---

1. Ask Questions

When you're assigned a literary essay in class, your teacher will often provide you with a list of writing prompts. Lucky you! Now all you have to do is choose one. Do yourself a favor and pick a topic that interests you. You'll have a much better (not to mention easier) time if you start off with something you enjoy thinking about. If you are asked to come up with a topic by yourself, though, you might start to feel a little panicked. Maybe you have too many ideas—or none at all. Don't worry. Take a deep breath and start by asking yourself these questions:

- **What struck you?** Did a particular image, line, or scene linger in your mind for a long time? If it fascinated you, chances are you can draw on it to write a fascinating essay.

- **What confused you?** Maybe you were surprised to see a character act in a certain way, or maybe you didn't understand why the book ended the way it did. Confusing moments in a work of literature are like a loose thread in a sweater: if you pull on it, you can unravel the entire thing. Ask yourself why the author chose to write about that character or scene the way he or she did and you might tap into some important insights about the work as a whole.

- **Did you notice any patterns?** Is there a phrase that the main character uses constantly or an image that repeats throughout the book? If you can figure out how that pattern weaves through the work and what the significance of that pattern is, you've almost got your entire essay mapped out.

- **Did you notice any contradictions or ironies?** Great works of literature are complex; great literary essays recognize and explain those complexities. Maybe the title (*Happy Days*) totally disagrees with the book's subject matter (hungry orphans dying in the woods). Maybe the main character acts one way around his family and a completely different way around his friends and associates. If you can find a way to explain a work's contradictory elements, you've got the seeds of a great essay.

At this point, you don't need to know exactly what you're going to say about your topic; you just need a place to begin your exploration. You can help direct your reading and brainstorming by formulating your topic as a *question,* which you'll then try to answer in your essay. The best questions invite critical debates and discussions, not just a rehashing of the summary. Remember, you're looking for something you can *prove or argue* based on evidence you find in the text. Finally, remember to keep the scope of your question in mind: is this a topic you can adequately address within the word or page limit you've been given? Conversely, is this a topic big enough to fill the required length?

GOOD QUESTIONS

> *"Are Romeo and Juliet's parents responsible for the deaths of their children?"*
> *"Why do pigs keep showing up in* LORD OF THE FLIES*?"*
> *"Are Dr. Frankenstein and his monster alike? How?"*

BAD QUESTIONS

> *"What happens to Scout in* TO KILL A MOCKINGBIRD*?"*
> *"What do the other characters in* JULIUS CAESAR *think about Caesar?"*
> *"How does Hester Prynne in* THE SCARLET LETTER *remind me of my sister?"*

---

2. COLLECT EVIDENCE

Once you know what question you want to answer, it's time to scour the book for things that will help you answer the question. Don't worry if you don't know what you want to say yet—right now you're just collecting ideas and material and letting it all percolate. Keep track of passages, symbols, images, or scenes that deal with your topic. Eventually, you'll start making connections between these examples and your thesis will emerge.

Here's a brief summary of the various parts that compose each and every work of literature. These are the elements that you will analyze in your essay, and which you will offer as evidence to support your arguments. For more on the parts of literary works, see the Glossary of Literary Terms at the end of this section.

LITERARY ANALYSIS

ELEMENTS OF STORY   These are the *what*s of the work—what happens, where it happens, and to whom it happens.

- **Plot:** All of the events and actions of the work.
- **Character:** The people who act and are acted upon in a literary work. The main character of a work is known as the *protagonist*.
- **Conflict:** The central tension in the work. In most cases, the protagonist wants something, while opposing forces (antagonists) hinder the protagonist's progress.
- **Setting:** When and where the work takes place. Elements of setting include location, time period, time of day, weather, social atmosphere, and economic conditions.
- **Narrator:** The person telling the story. The narrator may straightforwardly report what happens, convey the subjective opinions and perceptions of one or more characters, or provide commentary and opinion in his or her own voice.
- **Themes:** The main idea or message of the work—usually an abstract idea about people, society, or life in general. A work may have many themes, which may be in tension with one another.

ELEMENTS OF STYLE   These are the *how*s—how the characters speak, how the story is constructed, and how language is used throughout the work.

- **Structure and organization:** How the parts of the work are assembled. Some novels are narrated in a linear, chronological fashion, while others skip around in time. Some plays follow a traditional three- or five-act structure, while others are a series of loosely connected scenes. Some authors deliberately leave gaps in their works, leaving readers to puzzle out the missing information. A work's structure and organization can tell you a lot about the kind of message it wants to convey.
- **Point of view:** The perspective from which a story is told. In *first-person point of view*, the narrator involves him or herself in the story. ("I went to the store"; "We watched in horror as the bird slammed into the window.") A first-person narrator is usually the protagonist of the work, but not always. In *third-person point of view*, the narrator does not participate

in the story. A third-person narrator may closely follow a specific character, recounting that individual character's thoughts or experiences, or it may be what we call an *omniscient* narrator. Omniscient narrators see and know all: they can witness any event in any time or place and are privy to the inner thoughts and feelings of all characters. Remember that the narrator and the author are not the same thing!

- **Diction:** Word choice. Whether a character uses dry, clinical language or flowery prose with lots of exclamation points can tell you a lot about his or her attitude and personality.

- **Syntax:** Word order and sentence construction. Syntax is a crucial part of establishing an author's narrative voice. Ernest Hemingway, for example, is known for writing in very short, straightforward sentences, while James Joyce characteristically wrote in long, incredibly complicated lines.

- **Tone:** The mood or feeling of the text. Diction and syntax often contribute to the tone of a work. A novel written in short, clipped sentences that use small, simple words might feel brusque, cold, or matter-of-fact.

- **Imagery:** Language that appeals to the senses, representing things that can be seen, smelled, heard, tasted, or touched.

- **Figurative language:** Language that is not meant to be interpreted literally. The most common types of figurative language are *metaphors* and *similes,* which compare two unlike things in order to suggest a similarity between them— for example, "All the world's a stage," or "The moon is like a ball of green cheese." (Metaphors say one thing *is* another thing; similes claim that one thing is *like* another thing.)

---

3. CONSTRUCT A THESIS

When you've examined all the evidence you've collected and know how you want to answer the question, it's time to write your thesis statement. A *thesis* is a claim about a work of literature that needs to be supported by evidence and arguments. The thesis statement is the heart of the literary essay, and the bulk of your paper will be spent trying to prove this claim. A good thesis will be:

- **Arguable.** "*The Great Gatsby* describes New York society in the 1920s" isn't a thesis—it's a fact.

- **Provable through textual evidence**. "*Hamlet* is a confusing but ultimately very well-written play" is a weak thesis because it offers the writer's personal opinion about the book. Yes, it's arguable, but it's not a claim that can be proved or supported with examples taken from the play itself.

- **Surprising**. "Both George and Lenny change a great deal in *Of Mice and Men*" is a weak thesis because it's obvious. A really strong thesis will argue for a reading of the text that is not immediately apparent.

- **Specific**. "Dr. Frankenstein's monster tells us a lot about the human condition" is *almost* a really great thesis statement, but it's still too vague. What does the writer mean by "a lot"? *How* does the monster tell us so much about the human condition?

Good Thesis Statements

Question: In *Romeo and Juliet*, which is more powerful in shaping the lovers' story: fate or foolishness?

Thesis: "Though Shakespeare defines Romeo and Juliet as 'star-crossed lovers' and images of stars and planets appear throughout the play, a closer examination of that celestial imagery reveals that the stars are merely witnesses to the characters' foolish activities and not the causes themselves."

Question: How does the bell jar function as a symbol in Sylvia Plath's *The Bell Jar*?

Thesis: "A bell jar is a bell-shaped glass that has three basic uses: to hold a specimen for observation, to contain gases, and to maintain a vacuum. The bell jar appears in each of these capacities in *The Bell Jar*, Plath's semi-autobiographical novel, and each appearance marks a different stage in Esther's mental breakdown."

Question: Would Piggy in *The Lord of the Flies* make a good island leader if he were given the chance?

Thesis: "Though the intelligent, rational, and innovative Piggy has the mental characteristics of a good leader, he ultimately lacks the social skills necessary to be an effective one. Golding emphasizes this point by giving Piggy a foil in the charismatic Jack, whose magnetic personality allows him to capture and wield power effectively, if not always wisely."

4. DEVELOP AND ORGANIZE ARGUMENTS

The reasons and examples that support your thesis will form the middle paragraphs of your essay. Since you can't really write your thesis statement until you know how you'll structure your argument, you'll probably end up working on steps 3 and 4 at the same time.

There's no single method of argumentation that will work in every context. One essay prompt might ask you to compare and contrast two characters, while another asks you to trace an image through a given work of literature. These questions require different kinds of answers and therefore different kinds of arguments. Below, we'll discuss three common kinds of essay prompts and some strategies for constructing a solid, well-argued case.

TYPES OF LITERARY ESSAYS

- **Compare and contrast**

  Compare and contrast the characters of Huck and Jim in THE ADVENTURES OF HUCKLEBERRY FINN.

  Chances are you've written this kind of essay before. In an academic literary context, you'll organize your arguments the same way you would in any other class. You can either go *subject by subject* or *point by point*. In the former, you'll discuss one character first and then the second. In the latter, you'll choose several traits (attitude toward life, social status, images and metaphors associated with the character) and devote a paragraph to each. You may want to use a mix of these two approaches—for example, you may want to spend a paragraph a piece broadly sketching Huck's and Jim's personalities before transitioning into a paragraph or two that describes a few key points of comparison. This can be a highly effective strategy if you want to make a counterintuitive argument—that, despite seeming to be totally different, the two objects being compared are actually similar in a very important way (or vice versa). Remember that your essay should reveal something fresh or unexpected about the text, so think beyond the obvious parallels and differences.

- **Trace**

  Choose an image—for example, birds, knives, or eyes—and trace that image throughout MACBETH.

  Sounds pretty easy, right? All you need to do is read the play, underline every appearance of a knife in *Macbeth,* and then list them in your essay in the order they appear, right? Well, not exactly. Your teacher doesn't want a simple catalog of examples. He or she wants to see you make *connections* between those examples—that's the difference between summarizing and analyzing. In the *Macbeth* example above, think about the different contexts in which knives appear in the play and to what effect. In *Macbeth,* there are real knives and imagined knives; knives that kill and knives that simply threaten. Categorize and classify your examples to give them some order. Finally, always keep the overall effect in mind. After you choose and analyze your examples, you should come to some greater understanding about the work, as well as your chosen image, symbol, or phrase's role in developing the major themes and stylistic strategies of that work.

- **Debate**

  Is the society depicted in 1984 good for its citizens?

  In this kind of essay, you're being asked to debate a moral, ethical, or aesthetic issue regarding the work. You might be asked to judge a character or group of characters (*Is Caesar responsible for his own demise?*) or the work itself (*Is* JANE EYRE *a feminist novel?*). For this kind of essay, there are two important points to keep in mind. First, don't simply base your arguments on your personal feelings and reactions. Every literary essay expects you to read and analyze the work, so search for evidence in the text. What do characters in *1984* have to say about the government of Oceania? What images does Orwell use that might give you a hint about his attitude toward the government? As in any debate, you also need to make sure that you define all the necessary terms before you begin to argue your case. What does it mean to be a "good" society? What makes a novel "feminist"? You should define your terms right up front, in the first paragraph after your introduction.

  Second, remember that strong literary essays make contrary and surprising arguments. Try to think outside the box. In the *1984* example above, it seems like the obvious answer would be no, the totalitarian society depicted in Orwell's novel is *not* good for its citizens. But can you think of any arguments for the opposite side? Even if your final assertion is that the novel depicts a cruel, repressive, and therefore harmful society, acknowledging and responding to the counterargument will strengthen your overall case.

5. WRITE THE INTRODUCTION

Your introduction sets up the entire essay. It's where you present your topic and articulate the particular issues and questions you'll be addressing. It's also where you, as the writer, introduce yourself to your readers. A persuasive literary essay immediately establishes its writer as a knowledgeable, authoritative figure.

An introduction can vary in length depending on the overall length of the essay, but in a traditional five-paragraph essay it should be no longer than one paragraph. However long it is, your introduction needs to:

- **Provide any necessary context.** Your introduction should situate the reader and let him or her know what to expect. What book are you discussing? Which characters? What topic will you be addressing?

- **Answer the "So what?" question.** Why is this topic important, and why is your particular position on the topic noteworthy? Ideally, your introduction should pique the reader's interest by suggesting how your argument is surprising or otherwise counterintuitive. Literary essays make unexpected connections and reveal less-than-obvious truths.

- **Present your thesis.** This usually happens at or very near the end of your introduction.

- **Indicate the shape of the essay to come.** Your reader should finish reading your introduction with a good sense of the scope of your essay as well as the path you'll take toward proving your thesis. You don't need to spell out every step, but you do need to suggest the organizational pattern you'll be using.

Your introduction should not:

- **Be vague.** Beware of the two killer words in literary analysis: *interesting* and *important*. Of course the work, question, or example is interesting and important—that's why you're writing about it!

- **Open with any grandiose assertions.** Many student readers think that beginning their essays with a flamboyant statement such as, "Since the dawn of time, writers have been fascinated with the topic of free will," makes them sound important and commanding. You know what? It actually sounds pretty amateurish.

- **Wildly praise the work.** Another typical mistake student writers make is extolling the work or author. Your teacher doesn't need to be told that "Shakespeare is perhaps the greatest writer in the English language." You can mention a work's reputation in passing—by referring to *The Adventures of Huckleberry Finn* as "Mark Twain's enduring classic," for example—but don't make a point of bringing it up unless that reputation is key to your argument.

- **Go off-topic.** Keep your introduction streamlined and to the point. Don't feel the need to throw in all kinds of bells and whistles in order to impress your reader—just get to the point as quickly as you can, without skimping on any of the required steps.

---

6. WRITE THE BODY PARAGRAPHS

Once you've written your introduction, you'll take the arguments you developed in step 4 and turn them into your body paragraphs. The organization of this middle section of your essay will largely be determined by the argumentative strategy you use, but no matter how you arrange your thoughts, your body paragraphs need to do the following:

- **Begin with a strong topic sentence.** Topic sentences are like signs on a highway: they tell the reader where they are and where they're going. A good topic sentence not only alerts readers to what issue will be discussed in the following paragraph but also gives them a sense of what argument will be made *about* that issue. "Rumor and gossip play an important role in *The Crucible*" isn't a strong topic sentence because it doesn't tell us very much. "The community's constant gossiping creates an environment that allows false accusations to flourish" is a much stronger topic sentence— it not only tells us *what* the paragraph will discuss (gossip) but *how* the paragraph will discuss the topic (by showing how gossip creates a set of conditions that leads to the play's climactic action).

- **Fully and completely develop a single thought.** Don't skip around in your paragraph or try to stuff in too much material. Body paragraphs are like bricks: each individual one needs to be strong and sturdy or the entire structure will collapse. Make sure you have really proven your point before moving on to the next one.

- **Use transitions effectively.** Good literary essay writers know that each paragraph must be clearly and strongly linked to the material around it. Think of each paragraph as a response to the one that precedes it. Use transition words and phrases such as *however, similarly, on the contrary, therefore,* and *furthermore* to indicate what kind of response you're making.

---

7. WRITE THE CONCLUSION

Just as you used the introduction to ground your readers in the topic before providing your thesis, you'll use the conclusion to quickly summarize the specifics learned thus far and then hint at the broader implications of your topic. A good conclusion will:

- **Do more than simply restate the thesis.** If your thesis argued that *The Catcher in the Rye* can be read as a Christian allegory, don't simply end your essay by saying, "And that is why *The Catcher in the Rye* can be read as a Christian allegory." If you've constructed your arguments well, this kind of statement will just be redundant.

- **Synthesize the arguments, not summarize them.** Similarly, don't repeat the details of your body paragraphs in your conclusion. The reader has already read your essay, and chances are it's not so long that they've forgotten all your points by now.

- **Revisit the "So what?" question.** In your introduction, you made a case for why your topic and position are important. You should close your essay with the same sort of gesture. What do your readers know now that they didn't know before? How will that knowledge help them better appreciate or understand the work overall?

- **Move from the specific to the general.** Your essay has most likely treated a very specific element of the work—a single character, a small set of images, or a particular passage. In your conclusion, try to show how this narrow discussion has wider implications for the work overall. If your essay on *To Kill a Mockingbird* focused on the character of Boo Radley, for example, you might want to include a bit in your conclusion about how he fits into the novel's larger message about childhood, innocence, or family life.

- **Stay relevant.** Your conclusion should suggest new directions of thought, but it shouldn't be treated as an opportunity to pad your essay with all the extra, interesting ideas you came up with during your brainstorming sessions but couldn't fit into the essay proper. Don't attempt to stuff in unrelated queries or too many abstract thoughts.

- **Avoid making overblown closing statements.** A conclusion should open up your highly specific, focused discussion, but it should do so without drawing a sweeping lesson about life or human nature. Making such observations may be part of the point of reading, but it's almost always a mistake in essays, where these observations tend to sound overly dramatic or simply silly.

A+ Essay Checklist

Congratulations! If you've followed all the steps we've outlined above, you should have a solid literary essay to show for all your efforts. What if you've got your sights set on an A+? To write the kind of superlative essay that will be rewarded with a perfect grade, keep the following rubric in mind. These are the qualities that teachers expect to see in a truly A+ essay. How does yours stack up?

- ✓ Demonstrates a thorough understanding of the book
- ✓ Presents an original, compelling argument
- ✓ Thoughtfully analyzes the text's formal elements
- ✓ Uses appropriate and insightful examples
- ✓ Structures ideas in a logical and progressive order
- ✓ Demonstrates a mastery of sentence construction, transitions, grammar, spelling, and word choice

LITERARY ANALYSIS

Suggested Essay Topics

1. *How do Julie Morrel and Emmanuel Herbaut redeem humanity in Monte Cristo's eyes?*

2. *Compare Valentine de Villefort and Eugénie Danglars. In what ways do these characters act as foils for one another?*

3. *Edmond Dantès assumes a number of aliases during the course of the novel, and many other characters have a variety of different names as well. What do you consider to be the significance of names in* THE COUNT OF MONTE CRISTO? *What do you think is the significance of each of Edmond Dantès's assumed names?*

4. *Compare Madame Danglars and Mercédès. In what ways do these characters act as foils for each other?*

5. *What is the effect of Haydée's love for Monte Cristo?*

A+ Student Essay

In what sense is Abbé Faria Dantès's second father?

Of all the people Edmond Dantès encounters in *The Count of Monte Cristo,* his fellow prisoner in Château d'If, the Italian priest Abbé Faria, exerts perhaps the strongest influence on him. When Faria first meets Dantès, he finds a man full of despair and wrath who has been practically left for dead. Yet in the space of a few chapters (which span several years), Faria revives Dantès, giving him a renewed interest in life as well as a love of knowledge, a commitment to action, and a thirst for revenge. Faria not only revives the younger man, he also transmits his thoughts, beliefs, and even his experiences to Dantès, and in so doing, becomes a kind of father to Dantès.

Faria is most like a father to Dantès in that he gives the younger man symbolic life by instilling him with hope. His dramatic effect on Dantès is exemplified in the earliest moments of their relationship. Simply hearing Faria scratching from the adjoining cell makes Dantès abandon his morose, passive resolution to starve himself to death, which he quickly replaces with a vibrant, resourceful willfulness. Dantès becomes figuratively reborn through his contact with Faria, a metaphor Dumas emphasizes by having Faria emerge headlong from a hole the two men dig in the wall. Dantès begins to behave like a newborn animal, watching Faria closely and quickly adopting the old priest's behavior. He shows his willingness to establish filial ties with the older man implicitly, by rushing at him with love and gratitude, as well as explicitly, by declaring that he shall love Faria as he loves his father.

Faria extends his paternal role by leaving Dantès both material and spiritual legacies. He bequeaths Dantès the treasure of Monte Cristo, as a father might will the family fortune to an eldest son. He also transfers to Dantès his love of learning and philosophy, giving the younger man lessons in languages, sciences, and behavior just as a parent instructs a child. Dantès reinforces this parent-child dynamic by aping Faria's every movement and mannerism with the "imitative powers bestowed on him by nature." Years spent in solitary confinement have turned the broken, distraught Dantès into a blank slate, ready to receive Faria's imprint, and the lessons he absorbs reflect the ways in which knowledge is traditionally transmitted from one generation to the next.

In this light, the notion that Faria epitomizes the eighteenth-century rational philosopher while Dantès embodies the Romantic spirit of the nineteenth century seems especially apt. Just as the eighteenth-century belief in the power of science, reason, and social organization gave birth to the nineteenth-century spirit of Romanticism, which valued subjective experience and spirited heroes, the rational and understated Faria gives birth to the exotic and extravagant Count of Monte Cristo, who in his new incarnation seems almost like a superhero.

In addition to giving Dantès new life and providing him with the mental and material resources to prosper, Faria becomes Dantès's father by giving the younger man a guiding purpose in life: vengeance. Dantès's life gains a new meaning and sense of direction once he can focus his actions and talents in the quest of a single goal. By revealing the conspirators' plot to sabotage Dantès, the worldly Faria resembles a father introducing his naïve, innocent son to the harsh truths of the real world. This revelation acts as a socializing force on Dantès, as he begins to realize that he doesn't exist in a vacuum and therefore cannot pursue his goals without considering that other people's goals might conflict with his, causing them to take measures against him. Unfortunately, this viewpoint causes the value of human life to diminish in Dantès's eyes, and as a result he becomes willing to sacrifice others in the service of own goals—a practice reflected in his growing insistence on killing their prison guard to achieve their freedom.

Whether for good or bad, Faria becomes a father to Dantès due to the fact that, through his influence, he is the primary author of the young man's actions. In some ways, Faria may be a truer father to Dantès than his biological one. After all, rather than try to hide the unpleasantries of the world from his son—as Louis Dantès does when he downplays the way he has starved himself to pay his son's debt to Caderousse—Faria casts a bright light on the darker side of humanity. And though he immediately regrets having revealed Danglars's scheme against Dantès, Faria ultimately helps Dantès grow and ascertain the truly good by understanding the nature of evil.

LITERARY ANALYSIS

GLOSSARY OF LITERARY TERMS

ANTAGONIST

The entity that acts to frustrate the goals of the *protagonist*. The antagonist is usually another *character* but may also be a non-human force.

ANTIHERO / ANTIHEROINE

A *protagonist* who is not admirable or who challenges notions of what should be considered admirable.

CHARACTER

A person, animal, or any other thing with a personality that appears in a *narrative*.

CLIMAX

The moment of greatest intensity in a text or the major turning point in the *plot*.

CONFLICT

The central struggle that moves the *plot* forward. The conflict can be the *protagonist*'s struggle against fate, nature, society, or another person.

FIRST-PERSON POINT OF VIEW

A literary style in which the *narrator* tells the story from his or her own *point of view* and refers to himself or herself as "I." The narrator may be an active participant in the story or just an observer.

HERO / HEROINE

The principal *character* in a literary work or *narrative*.

IMAGERY

Language that brings to mind sense-impressions, representing things that can be seen, smelled, heard, tasted, or touched.

MOTIF

A recurring idea, structure, contrast, or device that develops or informs the major *themes* of a work of literature.

NARRATIVE

A story.

NARRATOR

The person (sometimes a *character*) who tells a story; the *voice* assumed by the writer. The narrator and the author of the work of literature are not the same person.

PLOT

The arrangement of the events in a story, including the sequence in which they are told, the relative emphasis they are given, and the causal connections between events.

POINT OF VIEW

The *perspective* that a *narrative* takes toward the events it describes.

PROTAGONIST

The main *character* around whom the story revolves.

SETTING

The location of a *narrative* in time and space. Setting creates mood or atmosphere.

SUBPLOT

A secondary *plot* that is of less importance to the overall story but may serve as a point of contrast or comparison to the main plot.

SYMBOL

An object, *character,* figure, or color that is used to represent an abstract idea or concept. Unlike an *emblem,* a symbol may have different meanings in different contexts.

SYNTAX

The way the words in a piece of writing are put together to form lines, phrases, or clauses; the basic structure of a piece of writing.

THEME

A fundamental and universal idea explored in a literary work.

TONE

The author's attitude toward the subject or *characters* of a story or poem or toward the reader.

VOICE

An author's individual way of using language to reflect his or her own personality and attitudes. An author communicates voice through *tone, diction,* and *syntax.*

LITERARY ANALYSIS

A NOTE ON PLAGIARISM

Plagiarism—presenting someone else's work as your own—rears its ugly head in many forms. Many students know that copying text without citing it is unacceptable. But some don't realize that even if you're not quoting directly, but instead are paraphrasing or summarizing, *it is plagiarism* unless you cite the source.

Here are the most common forms of plagiarism:

- Using an author's phrases, sentences, or paragraphs without citing the source
- Paraphrasing an author's ideas without citing the source
- Passing off another student's work as your own

How do you steer clear of plagiarism? You should *always* acknowledge all words and ideas that aren't your own by using quotation marks around verbatim text or citations like footnotes and endnotes to note another writer's ideas. For more information on how to give credit when credit is due, ask your teacher for guidance or visit www.sparknotes.com.

REVIEW & RESOURCES

QUIZ

1. What is Edmond Dantès's profession at the beginning of the novel?

    A. Soldier
    B. Tailor
    C. Sailor
    D. Lawyer

2. Who is the first person Dantès visits when he reaches Marseilles?

    A. His father
    B. Caderousse
    C. Mercédès
    D. Danglars

3. Which of the following statements is closest to the truth?

    A. Fernand Mondego envies Dantès's successful career, while Danglars envies Dantès's relationship with Mercédès.
    B. Fernand Mondego envies Dantès's relationship with Mercédès, while Danglars envies Dantès's successful career.
    C. Fernand Mondego envies Dantès's close relationship with his father, while Danglars envies Dantès's close relationship with Caderousse.
    D. Fernand Mondego envies Dantès's close relationship with Caderousse, while Danglars envies Dantès's close relationship with his father.

4. What does Danglars write in his letter to the public prosecutor?

    A. That Dantès is a soldier in Napoleon Bonaparte's army
    B. That Dantès is a powerful Jacobin
    C. That Dantès is a revolutionary spy
    D. That Dantès is bearing a letter that contains a revolutionary Bonapartist plot

5. Why does Villefort sentence Dantès to life in prison?

    A. Because he hates all Jacobins
    B. Because he is secretly a revolutionary and is worried this fact will come to light
    C. Because his father is the revolutionary plotter to whom Dantès's letter was addressed, and Villefort is worried this fact will come to light
    D. Because he truly believes Dantès has broken the law

6. How does Dantès figure out that he has been framed?

    A. He figures it out himself after discovering his accusation letter.
    B. Villefort tells him.
    C. Abbé Faria deduces it.
    D. None of the above

7. Why does everyone believe that Abbé Faria is insane?

    A. Because he claims to have an enormous hidden treasure
    B. Because he believes so strongly in a united Italy
    C. Because he remains a priest even though he does not believe in God
    D. Because he refuses to speak to any of the other prisoners

8. Why does Dantès consider Faria his second father?

    A. Because Faria saves his life
    B. Because Faria educates him
    C. Because Faria makes him wealthy
    D. All of the above

9. How does Dantès escape from prison?

    A. He hides in Faria's shroud.
    B. He digs his way out using Faria's tools.
    C. He buys his way out with his enormous fortune.
    D. He tunnels out of his cell.

10. Where is the Faria's fortune hidden?

    A. In Faria's old house in Rome
    B. Beneath the prison
    C. On the island of Monte Cristo
    D. In the Vatican

11. Why does Dantès give Caderousse a valuable diamond?

    A. Because Caderousse seems to regret his part in Dantès's downfall
    B. Because he knows that this windfall will only lead to more heinous acts on Caderousse's part, and he is eager to catch him doing some foul deed
    C. Because Caderousse agrees to give the diamond to Louis Dantès
    D. He does not give him the diamond; Caderousse's wife steals it from Dantès

12. When Dantès saves Monsieur Morrel from ruin, how does he sign his letter?

    A. The Count of Monte Cristo
    B. Sinbad the Sailor
    C. Lord Wilmore
    D. Edmond Dantès

REVIEW & RESOURCES

13. Who is the Abbé Busoni?

   A. An Italian priest who acts as confessor to Abbé Faria
   B. An Italian priest who acts as tutor to Abbé Faria
   C. An Italian priest who recognizes Dantès as a convict
       but does not turn him over to the authorities
   D. An alter ego of Dantès

14. How does Dantès win Albert de Morcerf's trust?

   A. By saving him from bandits
   B. By lending him his carriage
   C. By telling him that he once knew his father
   D. By saving Mercédès from financial ruin

15. Why does Eugénie Danglars not want to marry Albert de
    Morcerf?

   A. Because she despises men
   B. Because she wants to be a free and independent artist
   C. Because she is in love with her friend, Louise d'Armilly
   D. All of the above

16. Why does Valentine Villefort not want to marry Franz
    d'Epinay?

   A. Because his father was a loyal royalist
   B. Because her grandfather despises him
   C. Because she is in love with Maximilian Morrel
   D. All of the above

17. What do Julie and Emmanuel prove to Dantès?

   A. That true gratitude is possible
   B. That it is possible to be satisfied with one's life
   C. Both of the above
   D. None of the above

18. Whose greed does Dantès exploit?

    A. Danglars's
    B. Bertuccio's
    C. Benedetto's
    D. Albert's

19. Which of the following people does not play a part in the revenge scheme against Villefort?

    A. Signor Bertuccio
    B. Benedetto
    C. Madame de Villefort
    D. Maximilian Morrel

20. How does Haydée help bring about Fernand Mondego's downfall?

    A. By seducing him and then blackmailing him
    B. By seducing his son
    C. By testifying against him
    D. By stealing his money

21. Why does Albert de Morcerf refuse to fight a duel with Dantès?

    A. Because he is a coward
    B. Because he refuses to fight a duel he knows he will lose
    C. Because his mother tells him Dantès's story
    D. Because Eugénie begs him not to

22. Why do Albert and Mercédès abandon all of their wealth?

    A. Because they want nothing to do with a fortune that has been acquired through treachery
    B. Because they have both sworn to donate all of their wealth to God if Albert survives his duel with Dantès
    C. Because Dantès offers them a larger fortune if they consent to leaving the old one behind
    D. Because they are both planning on entering religious orders that denounce earthly possessions

REVIEW & RESOURCES

23. Why does Maximilian long to kill himself?

    A.   Because his father has been dishonored
    B.   Because he has lost his fortune
    C.   Because he believes that Valentine is dead
    D.   Because his sister, Julie, has married his enemy

24. Why does Dantès allow Maximilian to believe that Valentine is dead?

    A.   To punish him for the sins of his father
    B.   Because Dantès also believes that she is dead
    C.   Because he believes one can only know true happiness after knowing true despair
    D.   To keep him focused on his military service

25. How does Dantès learn to feel normal human emotions again?

    A.   By rekindling his love for Mercédès
    B.   By acting as a father to Maximilian
    C.   By allowing himself to fall in love with Haydée
    D.   He never regains his normal human emotions

ANSWER KEY

1: C; 2: A; 3: B; 4: D; 5: C; 6: C; 7: A; 8: B; 9: A; 10: C; 11: A; 12: B; 13: D; 14: A; 15: D; 16: C; 17: C; 18: C; 19: D; 20: C; 21: C; 22: A; 23: C; 24: C; 25: C

Suggestions for Further Reading

CHARLTON, D. G. *The French Romantics.* Cambridge, UK: Cambridge University Press, 1984.

HEMMINGS, F. W. J. *The King of Romance.* London: Charles Scribner's Sons, 1979.

KELLY, LINDA. *The Young Romantics: Victor Hugo, Sainte-Beuve, Vigny, Dumas, Musset, and George Sand and Their Friendships, Feuds, and Loves in the French Romantic Revolution.* New York: Random House, 1976.

LUCAS-DUBRETON, J. *The Fourth Musketeer: The Life of Alexandre Dumas.* New York: Century Bookbindery, 1989.

ROSS, MICHAEL. *Alexandre Dumas.* London: David & Charles, 1981.

STOWE, RICHARD. *Alexandre Dumas (père).* Boston: Twayne Publishing, 1976.

SparkNotes Literature Guides

Visit sparknotes.com for many more!